Divination

An Essential Guide to Astrology, Numerology, Tarot Reading, Palmistry, Runecasting, and Other Divination Methods

Your Free Gift (only available for a limited time)

Thanks for getting this book! If you want to learn more about various spirituality topics, then join Mari Silva's community and get a free guided meditation MP3 for awakening your third eye. This guided meditation mp3 is designed to open and strengthen ones third eye so you can experience a higher state of consciousness. Simply visit the link below the image to get started.

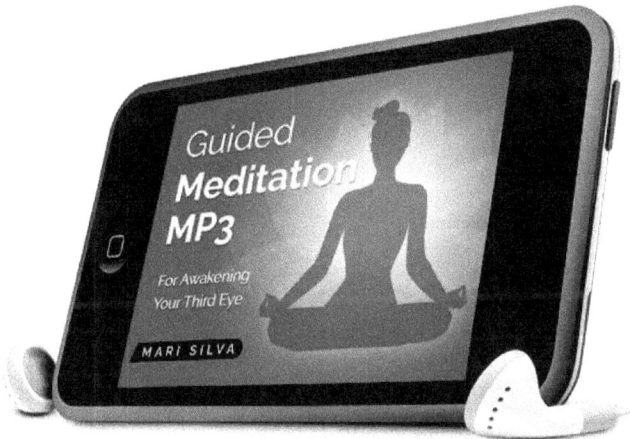

https://spiritualityspot.com/meditation

Contents

Introduction

Do you know what divination means? Do you ever wonder what you are destined for? Are you curious to learn about your future? Imagine if you could quickly sneak behind the curtain to see what is in store for you. Do you seek your true purpose in life? If you answered "Yes," here's some good news! When you harness the power of divination, you can unlock the secrets and mysteries of the cosmos. All the information you need to obtain this goal is presented in, *Divination: An Essential Guide to Astrology, Numerology, Tarot Reading, Palmistry, Runecasting, and Other Divination Methods.*

Divination is the art or practice of seeking knowledge about the future or the unknown. The concept is not a recent practice. It can help you understand the hidden significance or the fundamental cause of events in your life, and it can be used to foretell the future. Ancient cultures across the world have their own traditions and practices to understand the divine or the unknown. They use this information to make sense of everyday events. Do you want to learn how to do this? Well, this book will act as your guide every step of the way while you explore the fascinating world of divination and all that it entails.

You will learn about simple and effective time-honored techniques used to strengthen your intuition and harness universal energy. When you access your unconscious and use divination, you can lift the veil between the realms to peek into the future.

You will learn what divination means, the different tools to use, and how you can use it to sneak a glance at the future. Not only that, this book will introduce you to the basics of astrology and how to read a birth chart in an easy to understand manner. This will act as your introductory guide to using divination tools such as numerology, palmistry, runecasting, and tarot reading. Learning about this is not only interesting but can be instructive. Knowledge is power, and once you are equipped with the information given in this guide, you will be able to determine your life's purpose much easier.

So, if you are ready to begin, turn the page!

Chapter One: Is It Really Possible to See the Future?

You can see the future now! You know how your life will take its course and where you will be in five years. You have untold riches at your feet and the ability to disappear at will. Sounds downright silly, right? Well, of course. No one can predict anyone's future. No diviner can firmly state what will happen to you in five years. Wait, so why is this entire book written about "divination"?

Well, because divination is not simply looking into a crystal ball and predicting some mumbo jumbo. It is not looking at tea leaves and telling you that you will have a great year ahead. Divination is not a science; it's the culmination of years of study and patient learning about human personality and how all aspects and factors tie in to make each person unique.

What is Divination?

Divination is not just a bunch of people sitting around a Ouija board, chanting random things and trying to summon the spirits. Though Ouija is very much a part of the practice of divination, the meaning of divination is basically "divining" or trying to ascertain the hidden causes or significance or meaning behind events in a person's life. This practice was born centuries ago. In today's context, it encompasses various methods—astrology, birth charts, tarot, runecasting, etc. Modern divination teachers and practitioners work more toward ascertaining the root causes and impact of past and present events on a person's personality.

Historical Significance of Divination

Ancient cultures such as India, Mesopotamia, Egypt, and China sought to find answers to everyday questions and understand the environmental phenomena occurring around them, like thunder and lightning, seasons, migratory activities, etc. Each culture had its specific manner of dealing with the divine or the unknown.

The Chinese used tortoise shells to read and decipher patterns. This led to the I Ching movement and the hexagrams associated with it. The Vikings favored rune stones, but the Romans had a rather gruesome method of observing the intestines spilled out of slaughtered livestock. The Aboriginals from Australia turned inward and studied inner space. Others, such as the Mexican Indians, made use of plants to study and record answers. In the Old Testament, there is a reference to a set of divine stones called Urim and Thummim, which were used to figure out the course of future events.

The widespread art of divination you see around you today is a recent development. In days gone by, this art was mostly limited to oral transmissions and cave drawings or carvings on rocks by shamans, healers, priests, prophets, etc. Only after the invention of the printing press did this knowledge of divination spread far and wide, from the ancient world into the developing world.

After the invention of paper by the Chinese and a primitive movable type created thousands of years ago, it became possible to increase literary output. The I Ching, one of the world's most respected divination systems, saw the light of the day by being put in print. Later on, Johann Gutenberg's printing press gave rise to a multitude of books, card decks, flyers, etc. As literacy grew and the world population exploded, many divination systems came into existence. The most popular and those with close connections to history include astrology, tarot, runes, numerology, and I Ching. They are also known as the "classic" divination systems. These divination systems weren't merely tools to predict silly and inane questions; they challenged people's world views, analyzed personalities, and helped everyone understand the universe and themselves better.

How to Interpret Divination

There are various schools of divination, which try to explain phenomena in their own manner. Here they are discussed briefly.

Inductive Divination

Divining things from the skies or stars is common now, but it dates back to ancient times. The early ancients used to look up to the heavens and decipher phenomena on Earth, such as weather changes or migratory patterns of birds. Lightning, clouds, and thunder were interpreted as gods being angry with humans. Weather-related disasters such as excessive rain, storms, hail, drought, and floods suggested divine control over these forces.

There is a concept known as "augury," which the ancients used to discover divine events and God's hand in nature. Sometimes, this practice was also used for rituals involving the flight of birds or sacrificing an animal. For example, the study of the liver, called "haruspicy," was used to discover the history of the creature being studied. This is akin to modern-day palmistry. There was a technique known as "scapulimancy," which is divination from a fire-cracked shoulder blade. This technique was used mostly in North America. As mentioned earlier, "tortoiseshell divination" originated in China. The Chinese ancients used to study the spirals and patterns on the shell of a tortoise and interpret them.

Interpretive Divination

In this technique, omens are studied rather than looking toward the heavens or studying animals and birds. This relies on a cause-effect scenario. Of course, events do occur randomly, too, which cannot be explained by logic, while to a certain extent, there is a cause behind every effect. Divination by studying fire and related aspects, known as "pyromancy," was one such technique. The accused would be tested or probed in front of a fire, and if the fire suddenly leaped out at them, their guilt would be "proven." This may seem highly unscientific now, but that was how things were in the days of yore. Another technique involved throwing objects into the fire and seeing how the fire reacted to it. Divination by studying water (hydromancy) was also practiced. Water was used to study and interpret reflections of objects in it.

Other related practices included cleromancy and geomancy, divination by "lots" and "maps," respectively. Frankly, these were strange practices. For instance, in cleromancy, the objects found on the person conducting the divination were used to assess and predict the person's current status and future. Dried intestines, a tooth, or a decayed piece of hair all held different meanings in the interpretation. Along with these objects, the diviner asked various questions designed to elicit a response from the asker. If the answers betrayed the question or veered off course at some point, the diviner would interpret it as being the cause of the problem.

In geomancy, most notably in Africa, along with maps, drawings, and lots, occult readings were also conducted on the person asking the question. The diviner would attempt to read and interpret the body signs of the person (phrenology). Dream interpretation was also used and called "oneiromancy."

Intuitive Divination

To perform this, the diviner or shaman uses trance states to "cure" or find solutions to the person's problems. This is done either by drugging the man or woman or using their own tribal techniques. Going into a trance could also involve occult, spirit possession, and speaking in a different language.

Sometimes incubation was also practiced. In Egypt, people thought that sleeping inside a sacred temple would mean being blessed by God. The ancient Maya civilization saw young girls thrown into a deep well. Those who managed to climb out were required to tell others about their messages while inside the well. Trances and possession are seen in modern-day divination as well. More often than not, the diviner has their "spirit" replaced by the one they are summoning. After the necessary questions and answers have been dealt with, they return to their original spirit.

An unfortunate byproduct of all this was the negative connotation attached to divination in the form of witchcraft. Innocent women were accused of being witches and burnt at the stake for no fault of their own, except perhaps they looked different or suffered from a mental illness or physical deformity. Ordeals were horrifying too. The accused would be thrown into open rivers or seas. The presumption was that if they survived, they were innocent. Similar things happened to those thrown into a fire or from a hilltop.

Today, there are numerous divination methods, namely astrology, birth charts, horoscopes, tarot cards, runes, etc. During the turn of the twentieth century, methods such as crystal gazing, chiromancy, necromancy, and palm reading flourished. As you might already know, divination has more to do with intuition and an overall reading of the person's personality, traits, quirks, and mental state—everything that makes them unique. The following chapters deal with popular methods of divination that you will study and learn.

Chapter Two: Tools of Divination

Some divination methods are more popular, some are obscure, and yet others still unknown. It depends on your preference, means, and interest! You can choose whatever tool you wish and make it work for you. It is not as if tarot is better than astrology, or runes are better than a crystal ball. It just has to be something that you are comfortable with.

Here are a few popular methods and tools for divination. You will study these in greater detail in the following chapters.

Runes or Runecasting

These have been used since ancient times as a method of communicating. Runes are small stones or symbols carved into wood or stone that are then deciphered and interpreted. Each rune has a meaning attached to it, such as wealth, prosperity, travel, negative issues and aspects, and so on. You can buy a set of runes or even carve a set out of wood. Store your rune stones or crystals in a cloth pouch, draw the runes out randomly, place them on a cloth on the ground, and ask your questions. There are several books and guides available on the Internet to help you interpret the results.

Tarot Cards

Tarot is one of the most commonly used divination methods and has been around for a long time. People usually think that tarot is used to predict their future, but just like other divination methods, tarot is a tool and guide to help you understand yourself better. Tarot has two types of cards: The Major Arcana and the Minor Arcana. The Major Arcana comprises twenty-two cards dealing with major life characteristics and situations. The Minor Arcana is made up of 56 cards, which represent everyday issues and feelings. There are various layouts and spreads to try out. Once you shuffle the deck, you can choose any of the spreads and get a reading from them.

Crystal Ball

The stuff of supernatural movies, right? A beaded, mysterious mystic sits before a crystal ball, gazes into it, and predicts something ominous for the person inquiring, which usually turns out to be true. However, in reality, this has nothing to do with predicting anything. As with the other methods, you need to study long and hard about the intricacies of crystal ball gazing and interpreting the results.

Angel Cards

Do not confuse these with tarot cards. Angel cards are used to invoke the blessings of angels in one's life. These cards are mostly positive and sunny in nature and provide insight into personal growth, wealth, relationships, love, etc. When you are doing an angel card reading, it behooves you to listen to your heart and connect it with the spirit of the angels. Focus your energy on positive outcomes.

Spirit Boards

Also known as Ouija boards, this is another staple of horror movies. Ouija boards contain letters of the alphabet, numbers one to nine, and words such as "yes," "no," "here," and "goodbye." If you wish to try this out, you place a finger or hand on a coin or planchette in the middle of the board and try to contact whomever you wish. This is still a very imprecise branch of divination, though. Be careful before trying anything like this. Things might go wrong fast!

Pendulum

A pendulum can also answer specific questions for you. It is a chain that has a cone-shaped crystal or stone attached to it. Dangle it over a parchment or vellum sheet with "yes" and "no" printed on it. Swing it and see where it settles. You can buy or make your own pendulum. This method is also popular when trying to guess the gender of an unborn child, using a jewelry chain with a wedding band placed on it.

Psychic Cup

This cup is used for reading tea leaves. The person asking the question must drink hot tea (loose tea) and leave a small amount at the bottom. The dregs contain the tea leaves, which is then swirled around and poured onto a saucer. There will be patterns and swirls on the saucer that the diviner interprets.

Palm Reading

One of the most ancient methods of divination, palmistry, involves the reading of the palms. Palms contain numerous lines and bumps, and each of the lines and the bumps has significance. Taken in conjunction with each other and various other lines, every individual can get their unique reading by the palmist. This requires a detailed and thorough analysis of the palm.

Astrology

Everyone is familiar with their sun signs, but astrology is not just about those. It encompasses a lot more. The rising sign, the moon sign, and the birth chart, along with the stars' and planets' positions at the time of your birth—degrees, angles, and cusp aspects—combine to form a complete picture of you and your being.

Numerology

Numbers have a profound effect on your life. Your life path number, name number, fate number, house number, expression number—each one tells a story about you. It is convenient, practical, and fun!

DIY Tools for New Diviners

If you think that the practice of divination is expensive and will burn a hole in your pocket, fear not! There are plenty of do-it-yourself tricks and tips available on the Internet to help you out. Here are just a few tools you can make for yourself.

Make Your Own Pendulum

1. Take a chain or thin rope. It can be any old chain you have at home.

2. Search for a ring or ring-shaped object. It must have a hole, so it can slide into the chain or rope easily.

3. Slide the ring into the chain and close it. If it is a rope, tie the ends securely. The ring must not fall off.

4. Test the pendulum out. Write "Yes" and "No" on a sheet of paper and place your arm over it, such that the pendulum is perpendicular to the sheet. You can decide on the movement interpretations; the left is "Yes," the right is "No," and the middle is "Unknown."

5. Think of a question. Say, "Is the rainbow multicolored?" Swing the pendulum over the paper and see where it lands. It should land at the predetermined answer. If not, you need to change your interpretations. Do this a few more times until the swing of the pendulum is regulated. Now you are free to ask any question.

How to Make Your Own Rune Set

The most common Runic alphabet is known as the Elder Futhark (covered more extensively later on). It is made up of twenty-four letters. Some runes in a set come blank—or are called "Wyrd runes." Do not think of these runestones as tools for predicting the future, but as something to guide you on the journey.

Materials: Runes are often made of naturally occurring materials, so they usually aren't expensive. You can choose between wood, stones, pebbles, old bones of animals who have died of natural causes, clay, etc. You can carve your runes on these materials easily.

You will need twenty-four pieces of whatever material you choose because the Elder Futhark is made up of twenty-four alphabets. They must be similar in size. Also, they should not be so big that you cannot hold them and work with them. Once you gather your materials, it's time to paint or carve the runes onto them!

To begin with runecasting, you need to find a peaceful spot and time when you are the most energized from within. Take a candle and light it. Pick out a rune, think about its meaning, meditate for a while, and pass it near the candle flame. Place it to the right on the cloth that you are using. Do the same with the other runes. Now, you are ready to begin reading!

Make Your Own Tarot Cards

Wow, isn't this wonderful? A set of your own tarot cards made out of old poker cards!

• Your supplies should include an old set of playing cards, white paper, glue, labels, a pen, and most importantly, tarot card details.

• Organize your cards by suits and put them in ascending order, beginning with Ace and ending with King. The Joker cards go in a separate pile.

• Cut out the paper to fit the cards. Make 54 pieces.

• Now, you have to write! Write out tarot information on each suit of cards. For example, for all Heart cards, write "Tarot suit Cups." Then make a brief note of what that symbolizes. In the case of Cups, it means "emotions, deeper feelings, love, relationships." For all Diamonds, it will be "Suit of Pentacles," all Spades will carry "Suit of Swords," and all Clubs are "Suit of Spades." Find out the meaning of these tarot suits in the books listed for you at the end of the chapter.

• Organize each of your suits in ascending order, beginning with the Ace and ending with the King. Every number has a meaning attached to it, which you will find in the books listed later on. Write the corresponding traits on the cards. For example, three stands for development, self-expression, and growth, while four means stability, solidity, and a foundation.

• Congratulations! Your deck is ready. You can attempt a reading now.

Book Recommendations to Help You Start Your Practice

- *A Practical Guide to the Runes: Their Uses in Divination and Magic* (Lisa Peschel)
- *Seventy-Eight Degrees of Wisdom: A Book of Tarot* (Rachel Pollack)
- *Divination for Beginners: Reading the Past, Present, & Future* (Scott Cunningham)
- *The Complete Idiot's Guide to Numerology* (Jean Simpson)
- *A Little Bit of Numerology: An Introduction to Numerical Divination* (Novalee Wilder)
- *Numerology and the Divine Triangle* (Faith Javane and Dusty Bunker)
- *The Easiest Way to Learn the Tarot – Ever!!* (Dusty White)
- *The Ultimate Guide to Tarot Card Meanings* (Brigit Esselmont)
- *365 Tarot Spreads: Revealing the Magic in Each Day* (Sasha Graham)
- *A Little Bit of Palmistry: An Introduction to Palm Reading* (Cassandra Eason)
- *Runes for Beginners: A Guide to Reading Runes in Divination, Rune Magic, and the Meaning of the Elder Futhark Runes* (Lisa Chamberlain)
- *Futhark: A Handbook of Rune Magic* (Edred Thorsson)
- *Runecaster's Handbook: The Well of Wyrd* (Edred Thorsson)
- *Rudiments of Runelore* (Stephen Pollington)
- *The Secret Code on Your Hands: An Illustrated Guide to Palmistry* (Vernon Mahabal)

Chapter Three: Understanding Astrology

Astrology is the study of how distant planets and stars influence lives on Earth. It is not just making silly predictions based on one's whims and fancies. It considers the position of the sun, planets, and stars to form a complete picture of a person and their personality, relationships, career paths, and other aspects.

The most common thing people usually ask and know is their "sun sign." Your basic everyday newspaper and popular columns usually consider only the sun sign because it is the most basic form of astrology. Sun sign astrology only requires your date of birth— sometimes just the month of birth. For a more accurate and better reading, you need to study each planet's and star's position at the time of your birth. Not just this, the House position, angles, degrees, cusps, aspects, etc., come together and present a detailed and accurate picture of you, your personality, career, relationships, attributes, etc.

All ancient cultures practiced their own version of astrology. Some of the oldest among these include the Vedic, Chinese, and Tibetan practices of astrology. This is not a definite science; even in Western astrology, you will find various interpretations and philosophies.

A common categorization that is based on the end result is as follows:

- *Mundane Astrology* — This branch deals with world events, current affairs, predictions about the economy and general political climate, etc.

- *Interrogatory Astrology* — This branch of astrology refers to the more commonly known method of making predictions and analyses about people

- *Natal Astrology* — This is what astrology is all about. Looking at a birth chart and calculating the position, angles, degrees, and aspects of planets and stars accurately at the precise moment of a person's birth and then making predictions based on this.

Noteworthy Facts About Astrology

- Astrology came into being before the Copernican revolution. It assumed that the Sun moved around the Earth.

- The term "zodiac" comes from a Greek term used to identify animal sculptures.

- Ancient Egyptians were the first to identify and name the constellations in the night sky.

- The Ancient Greeks created today's modern zodiac sign. The Babylonians also had twelve signs, similar to what exists today.

- A book written by Ptolemy, called *Tetrabiblos*, made it possible for the Greek zodiac to gain popularity among the ancient world.

- Do you know what "horoscope" means? It literally means "hour watch."

- Astrology is not just a mumbo jumbo of predictions. To create an accurate birth chart and horoscope, one needs to calculate the planet's angles using geometry principles!

- Ancient Romans used mnemonics to remember the long lists of fortunes or fortune headings to be recited for someone's horoscope reading.

- Almost all ancient civilizations, such as Egypt, America, Greece, and Rome, believed that the stars and planets influence human life.

- The Roman Emperor Augustus used to have his Capricornian profile etched onto coins.

- There is a branch of study known as meteorological astrology, which tries to predict the weather based on the zodiac.

- Astrologers say that almost all the mighty empires in the ancient world, such as Britain, Rome, Egypt, and Germany, flourished because they were under the influence of Aries, the sign associated with creativity and birth.

- Former U.S. First Lady Nancy Reagan used to have her horoscope read regularly!

Sun Signs

"What is my Sun Sign? What does it signify?" These are common questions most people have, and they associate astrology with only the Sun sign. To calculate this, you only need your month and date of birth—yes, it's that simple! It gives you a fair idea about your personality without digging deeper.

The Sun is at the center of the solar system, and similarly, your Sun sign puts you at the center. It not only provides an overall view of your traits and life path, but it also tells you about your core and basic personality and passions. This sign is your identity in life.

Your Sun as an Air Sign (Libra, Gemini, Aquarius)

You are an intelligent being who also loves to party, have fun, and generally have a good time. You love socializing and are often found at large gatherings. People love to be around you.

Your Sun as a Fire Sign (Aries, Leo, Sagittarius)

You are drawn to power and ambition. You are fiercely protective of your loved ones and friends and will go to any lengths to keep them from harm. You also enjoy physical activities and outdoorsy events!

Your Sun as an Earth Sign (Taurus, Capricorn, Virgo)

You are practical, committed, and love material comforts in life. You love having beauty and order around you.

Your Sun as a Water Sign (Cancer, Scorpio, Pisces)

You are an enigmatic and mysterious person, stubborn as a mule and deep as a lake. You are uncannily intuitive and go by your emotions and darker desires. You prefer intimate connections with people rather than large groups.

Moon Signs

The Moon is associated with the cool, calm, and silvery peace of the night. It relates more to your inner being, private desires, dreams, thoughts, etc. To calculate your Moon sign, you need a full date of birth, exact time, and year.

The Moon is the ruler of beauty and emotions. It reveals things that you keep hidden from most people and tell only very trusted people in your life, like deep feelings, sentiments, intimacy, etc. If the Sun brings out your outer mind, the Moon reaches into the subconscious mind.

Your Moon as an Air Sign (Gemini, Libra, Aquarius)

Any changing experience or life event is dealt with by evaluation and not mere emotionality. You feel in charge when you rationally think things through.

Your Moon is a Fire Sign (Aries, Leo, Sagittarius)

Your inner world is characterized by action and excitement. You feel most alive and open when you can express your ideas and feelings confidently, without straying into negativity.

Your Moon as an Earth Sign (Taurus, Virgo, Capricorn)

Stability and solidity are the cornerstones of your inner being. Any change in this pattern will lead to anxiety. You are happiest when you are working toward a productive goal.

Your Moon as a Water Sign (Cancer, Scorpio, Pisces)

You are deep, sensuous, mysterious, and highly emotional. You love having your feelings involved with something and also love to probe other people's feelings!

Rising Signs

These are also known as your Ascendant Signs because they rule the First House of your natal chart. This is the most significant portion of the chart astrologers look for and study. It represents your physical side, body, and how you seem to others. It also depicts a fine balance between your inner and outer sides. The Rising Sign determines your overall outlook toward life.

Your Rising Sign as an Air Sign (Gemini, Libra, Aquarius)

You are loquacious, inquisitive, mentally agile, and very friendly. You know exactly what you want from life and are deliberate with your movements and actions.

Your Rising Sign is a Fire Sign (Aries, Leo, Sagittarius)

You are driven by power and ambition, focused, detailed, and blunt with people. Your physical energy astounds others around you, and you shine with vitality.

Your Rising Sign as an Earth Sign (Taurus, Virgo, Capricorn)

You focus more on the luxuries and material aspects of life. You are to the point, dependable, and stable. Others look to you for guidance.

Your Rising Sign as a Water Sign (Cancer, Scorpio, Pisces)

You are very emotional, dark, sensitive, and lash out when hurt. You keep secrets hidden so well that you sometimes have trouble trusting any other person. You are also easily influenced by the environment.

What the Planets Mean in Astrology

We all know how planets travel in the sky. As they move through the different imaginary zodiac zones, their energies at any given point of time are different from those at other points in time. A birth chart is most helpful while giving out the exact time, angle, and degree of the planet and zodiac at your birth's precise time, giving you a unique reading. If you know what planets live in your birth chart, you can examine their relationships with the other planets, aspects, and signs and determine your personality and future.

Now study the interpretations of the planets in astrology.

Sun

As said earlier, the Sun is at the center of the solar system. It gives life to Earth, which is why the Sun signs are so important in astrology. The Sun represents creativity, positive vibes, purity, and life forces and is mainly the driving force behind everything we do. The Sun naturally rules Leo.

Moon

The Moon represents the feminine side —nurture, empathy, compassion, security, emotions, expressions, etc. It brings out the maternal side. There are certain parts of your personality that you do not like to show others. The Moon brings all that out. It shows you your need for security, protection, comfort, and emotional wellbeing. The Moon naturally rules Cancer.

Mercury

Mercury is, as you guessed it, mercurial! It is the planet for communication, intellect, multi-tasking, reasoning, and powers of expression. Usually, Mercury is associated with its topsy-turvy retrograde periods. But even so, it affects how you infer and transmit information, communicate, and what your travel and exploration style is. Mercury naturally rules Gemini and Virgo.

Venus

Venus is the planet of love, beauty, romance, sensuality, and everything to do with these aspects. No wonder writers and poets fawn over it! Named after the Greek goddess herself, this planet concerns itself with aesthetics, beauty in every form, and, surprisingly, money. It defines luxury in terms of expensive things and baubles, such as chocolates, trips, and jewels. Venus naturally rules Taurus and Libra.

Mars

Mars is usually associated with aggression and drive. It was named after the God of War, so naturally, it is full of raw drive, energy, temper, action, and fighting spirit. Mars shows you how to tackle problems in life and work toward your goals. It also lives up to its moniker, the Red Planet, by being associated with sexual aggression and intensity. Mars naturally rules Aries.

Jupiter

Jupiter is the planet representing optimism, good fortune, and abundance. This is the largest planet in the solar system and carries with it a great deal of positivity. It indicates positivity, growth, opportunity, and good vibes in general. It also represents philosophy, teaching, education, broadening of minds, etc. Jupiter teaches you to keep working toward your goals and dreams and not give up. Jupiter naturally rules Sagittarius.

Saturn

Tough old Saturn is all about life, lessons, code of conduct, discipline, criticism, and tough decisions. Just like the Moon is all about maternal instincts, Saturn is about paternal instincts. It represents challenges and restrictions, boundaries and limits, and roadblocks. These can feel suffocating but remember: There can be no easy way through life. Saturn naturally rules Capricorn.

Uranus

Uranus represents an awakening within oneself. This might happen due to an external or internal revelation or progress in life or just letting your subconscious mind do its job. It indicates forward thinking, creativity, and changes. These changes can be abrupt, leading to a completely different way and thinking pattern of life. Uranus is also thought of as a lightning bolt, which jolts a person awake from slumber and gives them deep insights. Uranus naturally rules Aquarius.

Neptune

This planet is all about your dreams, mystic realm, idealism, intuition, psychic dealings, and astral aspects. Neptune is a dreamy-eyed planet, ethereal and full of calming colors. It represents artistic expression, spirituality, meditation, escapism and works toward lifting a person from life's banalities into something outwardly! Neptune naturally rules Pisces.

Pluto

Pluto, having been downgraded to a dwarf planet, is still a tremendous force in astrology. It represents a brooding, dark mind, the underworld, occult, intensity, and moodiness in general. Pluto is intense and quiet, deep and dark. It represents the extremes — light and dark, day and night, ending and beginning. Pluto naturally rules Scorpio.

Zodiac Signs

There are four elements in astrology, each corresponding to three signs, making a total of twelve. These are Fire, Earth, Air, and Water. These elements act like building blocks of life. Now you will delve into the elements and how the signs are connected to them.

The Fire Element

Aries, Leo, and Sagittarius fall into this category. Fire signs signify assertion, candid behavior, and spontaneity. Fire is usually impulsive and does not reflect first. It also signifies passion, courage, creativity, and immense pride in one's work. An outer spirit most likely guides it. Fire signs are the life of any party. They are idealists and love to take the lead. For instance, Aries is innovative, enthusiastic, and always ready to take on challenges. Leo is a Fixed Fire sign; it is more loyal, passionate, and fierce. Such people make particularly good managers and teachers. Sagittarius is a Mutable Fire sign, which means it is more flexible, but it is also fiery when aroused. Such people do well in spiritual endeavors. Fire signs fall under the masculine aspect.

The Earth Element

Taurus, Virgo, and Capricorn fall under this category. Earth signs are known for their reliability, solidity, and practicality. They build things, collect valuables, are pragmatic and sensible, materialistic, and like to surround themselves with fine luxuries. They need to feel in control of their immediate physical environment. They also make excellent managers and administrators because it ties in beautifully with their ability to manage others, see results for themselves, and also keep others in some semblance of control! Earth signs are feminine.

The Air Element

Gemini, Libra, and Aquarius are Air elements. These signs are fun, curious, intellectual, and, most importantly, fair-minded. Air signs are socially active, excellent communicators, and humanitarian by nature. Libra is a Cardinal Air sign, Gemini is a Mutable Air sign, and

Aquarius is a Fixed Air sign. Of the three, Gemini is mostly adaptable to any situation. Libra thrives on action, comparing ideas and dreams and generally raring to go. Aquarius is the most steady and loyal of these signs. It tends to dwell on things rather than be impulsive and rash about decisions. Just like Fire signs, Air signs fall under the masculine category.

The Water Element

Cancer, Scorpio, and Pisces are Water Signs. As is their name, these signs are known for their intuitive powers, deep and emotional nature, and fluidity. Just like still waters run deep, these signs are emotionally deep and dark. They rely on intuition and gut feelings. Of the three, Cancer is caring, nurturing, and more focused on other people's feelings. Scorpio is magnetic, mysterious, psychic, and the keeper of all secrets. There is not much that escapes the canny Scorpio. Pisces is dreamy, spiritual, and full of starry dreams, compassionate to a fault, and easily influenced. Water signs are feminine and are very deep, private, stubborn, and highly secretive too. They do not see things on the surface level—they prefer to dig deep and find out the real meaning of things and feelings.

Now that you have a basic understanding of the effect of planets and stars on human beings on Earth take this knowledge forward to the next chapter and apply the principles and interpretations there.

Chapter Four: How to Read a Birth Chart

Most people love to read their horoscope, right? But have you ever wondered how the stars and planets foretell your story so succinctly? There must be something behind all that. To understand how a birth chart works and how to read one, you need to understand the basic concepts, as detailed in this chapter.

The Houses

What this means is the sky at the time of your birth. The houses are the backbone of the birth chart. In a typical birth chart, the left corner is known as the "ascendant" or rising. You read the chart from here and progress in an anticlockwise movement. Usually, there are twelve houses in a typical birth chart. Opposite to the ascendant is the "descendant" part of the setting.

The first house in the chart depicts your daily life areas: goals, self-esteem, appearance, behavior, etc.

The Signs

The signs depict the characteristics of the sky at the moment of a person's birth. What was the rising sign? What was the setting sign? What was the neutral sign? This is also where the individual aspects of every person's chart come to life.

The Planets

These are not just fiery heavenly bodies revolving and rotating in the sky. They can mirror the experiences and characteristics of people on Earth. Planets show the personality traits, strengths and weaknesses, and overall life path of a person.

So, how do you read a birth chart? By reading the major components listed above and other elements such as aspects, cusps, degrees, ascendants, and descendants.

Any basic birth chart comprises four elements: an individual's Sun, Moon, Ascendant, and Chart Ruler. So, look at the sign and house position of these four elements and try to read the birth chart accurately.

The Sun and Moon Elements

Not only are these the basic chart elements, but they also foretell a person's basic traits. The Sun concerns itself with the personality's expressive and masculine side, while the Moon is connected to one's innate self and feminine side. These two, like yin and yang, provide a wholesome picture of one's personality. Identify your Sun and Moon element in your chart with this symbology. The house and sign meanings will give you a picture of your inner and outer self.

Ascendant and Chart Ruler Elements

These two elements look toward the ongoing and upcoming phases in your life and shape your whole personality in the future. What your life experiences teach you is revealed by your Ascendant. This particular element is associated with the First House, and therefore, only has a sign attached to it, no aspect or planet.

Your Chart Ruler is the planet you are governed by. If you look at your Chart Ruler's or planet's sign and house position, it tells you much more about who you are and whom you may turn out to be. When looking at your birth chart, locate this planet, and look up the sign and house placement.

Aspects of the Chart

The associations that form between the mentioned components are called "aspects." For a detailed analysis of the birth chart, you must learn about the aspects detailed in this chapter. After that, look into the planetary readings. Just remember that the ones closest to the core of your chart will determine your personality and future. Those in the periphery are just faint layers of what makes you a whole human being. All in all, consider what you analyze in the First House, as that is a vital component of your entire being.

The Twelve Houses of the Zodiac

A typical birth chart is circular and divided into segments. The first wheel in the circle represents the twelve Houses of the zodiac and the second wheel represents the twelve signs of the zodiac. This is different for everyone, depending on where his or her house-cusp falls. Houses one to six are your "personal houses." Houses seven to twelve are known as "interpersonal houses." Each of these houses has its own planetary ruler and sign—and this is different for everyone. A general ruler of the chart and your own personal ruler of the chart might be entirely different. Now, look at what each house represents.

First House: Self

Ruled by: Aries and Mars

Interpretation: Also known as the "ascendant," the first house is all about you. What makes you—your self-esteem, goals, leadership, initiatives, and appearance. It ties in very strongly with all the beginnings and "firsts" in our life.

Second House: Finance and Value

Ruled by: Taurus and Venus

Interpretation: This is the house for physical and tangible things such as immediate physical environment, sensory experiences, property, possessions, and wealth. It also concerns itself with your attitude toward these things and the value you attach to things and yourself.

Third House: Communication

Ruled by: Gemini and Mercury

Interpretation: This deals with your method of expression and communication with the outside world. How you interact with people, experiences, places, and things fall into this gambit. It also governs how you use logic to your advantage, how you manage relationships within and outside the family, and how well or poorly you make your points.

Fourth House: Home

Ruled by: Cancer and the Moon

Interpretation: Quite literally the cornerstone of any person's life, this house is all about your foundation. It represents the home, family, parents, stability, nurturing, emotionality, comfort zones, and nostalgia. It also stands for the time in your life when you felt the happiest and the most secure, your memories, and sometimes ancestors.

Fifth House: Creativity and Pleasure

Ruled by: Leo and the Sun

Interpretation: This house is about fun! All of your creative pursuits, hobbies, passions, interests, romances, drama, affairs, etc., fall under this. It also represents children, luck, heart, and love.

Sixth House: Health and Service

Ruled by: Virgo and Mercury

Interpretation: Your work ethics, service to others, everyday tasks, organization, dedication to work, etc., come under this house. It also represents your health and lifestyle, diet, nutrition, exercise, and whether there is any personal quest for self-improvement.

Seventh House: Partnerships

Ruled by: Libra and Venus

Interpretation: This is opposite to the first house (Self). It naturally follows that this house is about service and connections with other people, instead of the self. It governs relationships, marriage, commercial partnerships, contracts, etc. In a converse direction, it can also represent negative partnerships like enemies, lawsuits, or divorces.

Eighth House: Sex and Transformation

Ruled by: Scorpio and Pluto

Interpretation: This house has a mysterious aura about it, no doubt because the ever-enigmatic Scorpio rules it! It represents death, dark sides, wills, investments, inheritances, occult, losses, sacrifices, and above all, transformation. Something begins when something ends. It's an inevitable cycle. This is a house of transformation and personal growth.

Ninth House: Big Ideas
Ruled by: Sagittarius and Jupiter

Interpretation: The third house reveals basic thought processes. The ninth house, opposite it, is all about higher thinking and philosophy. It represents adventure, travel, exploration, and a constant search for deeper meanings to life and challenges oneself for growth.

Tenth House: Public Image
Ruled by: Capricorn and Saturn

Interpretation: This is sometimes known as the "Midheaven" in astrology. How you cultivate your image in public, reputation, and life path are determined and revealed by this house. It connects itself with fame, tradition, honor, achievement, authority, and influences in your life and career path.

Eleventh House: Community and Friends
Ruled by: Aquarius and Uranus

Interpretation: This house is about groups, community, networking, friendships, teamwork, humanitarian causes, originality, astronomy, inventions, etc. It governs the need for social justice and a collective goal to achieve something better in life and contribute to society.

Twelfth House: Subconscious and Secrets
Ruled by: Pisces and Neptune

Interpretation: This represents the evolution of the soul. It depicts secrets, fantasies, desires, endings, karma, traumas, separation from society (imprisonment, institutionalization), paranormal and occult energies, old age, the afterlife, subconscious desires, etc.

Sister Signs of the Zodiac

Each sign of the zodiac corresponds to a different sign, and they might be opposites or share similarities. These signs also share modalities and congenial elements, as you will see in the following segment.

Modalities

In the Zodiac, Taurus, Leo, Aquarius, and Scorpio are known as the Fixed Signs. They are the most stable, stubborn, and deliberate signs.

Gemini, Sagittarius, Virgo, and Pisces are known as Mutable Signs. They are remarkably easygoing, flexible, and tend to go with the flow.

Aries, Capricorn, Libra, and Cancer are known as the Cardinal Signs. These signs are known for their bossy nature, and such people usually take the initiative much quicker than the other signs.

Elements of the Zodiac

Active Elements

The Air Signs (Gemini, Libra, and Aquarius) and the Fire Signs (Aries, Leo, and Sagittarius) are the active elements.

Passive Elements

The Earth Signs (Taurus, Capricorn, and Virgo) and Water Signs (Scorpio, Cancer, and Pisces) fall in this category.

Even though they might be polar opposites, Sister signs fulfill each other's weaknesses. Now see the sister sign pairings in the zodiac and understand their interpretations.

Aries (First, Cardinal, Fire) and Libra (Seventh, Cardinal, Air)

An Arian is almost always spontaneous and the life of the party. They can be volatile and hard to handle. They are also filled with excitement for new things in life. Libra is the total opposite. They are gentle, patient, warmhearted, and like to stay out of chaos. These two signs balance each other out and together make a strong team.

Taurus (Second, Fixed, Earth) and Scorpio (Eighth, Fixed, Water)

Taurus is a bull, stubborn and unyielding. So is Scorpio. Taurus loves beauty, taste, and class in his life. So does Scorpio. Taurus and Scorpio are both very intense signs. The difference lies in their way of processing these personality traits. Taurus is upfront and gives it back in a transparent manner. Scorpio bides their time and plans revenge carefully. Both signs are totally impervious to outside influences when it comes to their life and career.

Gemini (Third, Mutable, Air) and Sagittarius (Ninth, Mutable, Fire)

Gemini is all about gregariousness and knowing as much about the world as they possibly can. Such people are usually curious about all aspects of life, and others sound them. Sagittarius tries to make sense of the world. They are the kind of people that seek meaning and a greater purpose in life. Both signs are paired together because each can bounce off the other to gain a new perspective.

Cancer (Fourth, Cardinal, Water) and Capricorn (Tenth, Cardinal, Earth)

Cancer is mostly about care and nurture. This nursing and motherly instinct is very strong in this sign. They are also intuitive and introspect a lot, so they can usually tell when someone is feeling down or low. They will always be there for you and have your back. Capricorn, on the other hand, believes in tough love. When in relationships or forming strong feelings for someone, such people will feel responsible for that person. In their misguided zeal, they might try to steer the other person in the direction they feel is most appropriate. It works well with Cancer because, while both are caring types, Cancer will intuitively pull Capricorn out of tight spots.

Leo (Fifth, Fixed, Fire) and Aquarius (Eleventh, Fixed, Air)

Leo is fiercely protective and connects with people at a very basic level. Their emotions and actions will always tend toward the protective nature they possess. On the other hand, Aquarius also believes in love and protection, but at an emotional and mental level. A Leo connects more with the physical aspect; an Aquarius connects with the mind.

Virgo (Sixth, Mutable, Earth) and Pisces (Twelfth, Mutable, Water)

A Virgo is sensitive, honest, and values authenticity in all aspects of life. They value truth and transparency. A Virgo is also intelligent and stable. Unlike this, Pisces is a dreamy-eyed person, with loads of plans and activities bouncing in their heads. They live in castles of air most of the time. But even so, their imagination and creation make them fun to be with. Both the signs bounce off each other splendidly.

Now that you have covered the basics of houses, signs, and sister signs in the zodiac, it is time to delve a little deeper into the reading of a birth chart. You will study other factors such as aspects, angles, and cusps.

Planetary Aspects

The distance between any two planets and zodiac signs is known as the "aspect." Aspects are measured using geometry (degrees and angles). Seven major aspects are classified as "soft" and "hard." Soft aspects include conjunct, trine, and sextile. Hard aspects include semisextile, square, quincunx, and opposite.

The Seven Major Aspects

- Conjunct
- Semisextile
- Sextile
- Square
- Trine
- Quincunx
- Opposite

So, how does this work in a birth chart? For instance, if you find that Mercury and Venus appear in the chart with a soft aspect, this means their powers are blended, and you may have an excellent love interest and communication with that person on the horizon. Conversely, if the two planets form a hard aspect, you might struggle in either area.

Now, look at each of the aspects in brief detail.

Conjunct: Two Planets in the Same Sign (Zero Degrees Apart)

Such planets will blend their energies, form a powerful alliance, and boost the people within their ambit. For example, if you have Neptune and Mercury in this formation, this can mean an extremely creative person who is sometimes absentminded. If three or more planets are in conjunction, it is known as "stellium." The formation of the planets is also important. If it is Uranus or Mars, it might mean stress and tension for the person involved.

Semisextile: One Sign Apart (Thirty Degrees Separation)

These planets might not have anything in common, making the proximity a bit difficult. For example, if one planet is in Sagittarius, the other in Scorpio, look at what happens. Scorpio is a fixed water sign and highly emotional and introverted. Sagittarius is a mutable fire sign and extroverted. As long as these two are semisextile to each other, the discomfort will continue.

Sextile: Two Signs Apart (60 Degrees Separation)

This is a highly compatible situation. Though not strong individually, they bring with them cooperation and friendly interactions. Such a formation means a lot of compatibility factors for the individual. Pleasure, companionship, and camaraderie are promoted with this sextile. If two planets were sextile in your chart, that part of your life would be stress-free. It might be anything—your career, love life, marriage, or children.

Square: Three Signs Apart (90 Degrees Separation)

This is a classic tug-of-war situation, which is why this is one of the "hard" aspects. A battle of wills is almost always the consequence as neither planetary characteristic is willing to budge. For example, if Jupiter falls in Virgo, forming a square with Venus in Sagittarius, this might mean that your micromanaging tendencies are brimming to the hilt, obsessing over what everyone says to you. But that would also mean that with Venus in your Sagittarius, you rush off and indulge in impulsive romantic acts, which might not always be the best thing to do. If your natal chart has squares in it, that will reveal parts of your nature, which you need to reflect and work upon.

Trine: Four Signs Apart (120 Degrees Separation)

This is normally considered the best aspect since there is harmony, ease of interaction, and luck amongst the planets involved. Sharing the same elements promote the same goals and energies. If you spot a trine in your birth chart, look closely at what it says. A trine in stable earth elements makes you a solid, dependable person who is also a hard worker.

Quincunx: Five Signs Apart (150 Degrees Separation)

This is an eccentric angle, so to speak. This aspect denotes much awkwardness and discord because the signs have nothing in common and feel like strangers at a party. Major cooperative activities will need to be attempted if these signs are to work well together. For example, if Mercury lands in meticulous Virgo, it forms a quincunx with Mars in the impatient Aries. You already see the problem! Detail-oriented does not go well with "go with the flow." Such quincunxes have different interpretations. Some planetary formations make you take risks, others make you independent, some drive you crazy, and yet others might help you overcome your fears.

Opposite: Six Signs Apart (180 Degrees Separation)

These signs are polar opposites, the meeting of two extremes. Conflict is guaranteed, but so is balancing and mirroring of the signs and personalities. There is a reason why opposites attract. It's because of the tremendous learning potential the two offer each other. The strengths and weaknesses of each sign can be used to fulfill those of the other.

Cusps, Degrees, Signs, and Interceptions

One cannot talk about these three points in isolation; they have to be understood together. A cusp is not merely the overlapping point between two Sun Signs. At the moment of your birth, the Sun was in one sign. Because the Sun moves from sign to sign every year, the cusp actually means that imaginary lines separate the houses in the horoscope, not the signs.

Sometimes referred to as "angles," four of the cusps have different names.

- First House Cusp: Ascendant
- Fourth House Cusp: Nadir
- Seventh House Cusp: Descendant
- Tenth House Cusp: Midheaven

As you already know, the houses represent various areas of the sky. The first house is for the east, the seventh is for the western horizon, the tenth is for the highest point in the horizon at any given point, and the fourth is for its opposite point.

For example, if someone were born with twenty degrees of Sagittarius rising, it would mean that in the imaginary 360-degree clock or circle of houses, the first house hand points to the middle of the sign if someone were born near the equator and the second house hand points in the middle of Capricorn.

Now, say Sagittarius is on the cusp of both the first and second houses. This means that Capricorn is entirely omitted from the reading, and the third house gets Aquarius instead. This sort of situation is known as an "interception." Of course, this does not mean that Capricorn has vanished! It is merely hidden in the second house.

Planets are divided into two categories as per your planetary chart: outer and personal.

The outer planets of the chart are Jupiter, Saturn, Uranus, Neptune, and Pluto.

- Jupiter represents your personal and higher growth.

- Saturn represents integrity, rules, and ambitions.

- Uranus stands for your imagination.

- Pluto represents how ready you are for a change in your life.

Personal planets are the Sun, the Moon, Mercury, Venus, and Mars.

- The Sun tells you about your overall personality.

- The Moon tells you about what you think and feel.

- Mercury is all about your perceptions in life.

- Mars represents your ambition and willpower.

See where the planets appear in your birth chart and under which sign. For instance, if you see Uranus in Aries in the fourth house, it means the following:

- Uranus = growth, potential, imagination

- Aries = fiery, passionate, charming

- Fourth House = family, property, relationships

You now know that planets, stars, and their precise alignments combine to give you a holistic and complete picture of yourself. The answers to questions, sometimes, can indeed be found in your planetary position.

Chapter Five: Numerology — See Fate Unfold Through Numbers

Numerology — What Does It Mean?

A study of numbers in your life is called numerology. Each number conveys deep meaning. The field of numerology is universal, as numbers are universal in nature. Numerology isn't a stand-alone field. It ties in neatly with astrology and other similar divination methods. This field's basis lies in the fact that almost everything tangible in the universe can be broken down into the simplest form of numbers.

The History of Numerology

Some of the earliest numerology records come from Egypt, Babylon, Rome, China, and Japan. It is universally agreed that the great mathematician Pythagoras, also a Greek philosopher, first put forward radical ideas about numerology. Of course, it wasn't known by that name centuries ago. It was Dr. Julian Stenton who came up with the nomenclature.

Positive and Negative Numbers

Just as there are positive and negative integers on a number scale, numerology refers to the balance of positive and negative energies the numbers have on your life and other aspects related to it, such as career, relationships, and health.

Master Numbers

11, 22, and 33 are known as the master numbers in numerology. Taken together with the overall context, these numbers have deep meanings. As with any other divination form, you need to look at the holistic picture before interpreting anything. Usually, when the numbers totaled, if you are left with a double-digit number, say 52, 5+2 becomes 7. This gives you your primary number as 7. But if your total ends up being either 11 or 22 or 33, you don't add these up to get 2, 4, and 6. You let the master number be as it is.

Strengths and Weaknesses from Numbers

Numbers do reveal a lot about you, including what you are good at and what you need to work on. For many people, numerology provides their life's purpose!

Combinations of Numbers

When you look at the number chart and the traits associated with each number, you get a better sense of clarity as to why certain things happen to you. For instance, if you keep fighting with your best friend or sibling, if you do not share a warm relationship with your loved ones, or if you feel magnetically drawn toward someone, an in-depth look and analysis of the numerical relationships between you and your friends and family will reveal a lot!

Numerology and Your Birth

Sometimes, people change their birth name and hope to expect success and riches. It does not work that way. Sure, adding or removing letters from your name will change the numerology of your birth and life number, but when you were born, the alignment of the stars and planets, the angles and degrees they made, and your birth name all add up to a powerfully unique number to "make you."

Numerology — What Is It?

Basically, many calculations! It is not just simple addition, though. These calculations can involve several levels and sequences. Even basic reading involves a lot of hard work. After a detailed analysis, a numerologist can arrive at your birth number, life path number, soul urge number, expression number, etc. The following explains the meaning of each of the numbers first and then goes on to the other aspects of numerology.

Number 1: These people are usually at the top of their game. Leadership skills, charisma, initiative, and entrepreneurial spirit are associated with this number. Yes, such people also have little patience to deal with others and may sometimes come across as brash and arrogant. In matters of love and romance, 1s try to be alone for a long time before finding someone!

Number 2: They strike a delicate balance between all areas in their life. They crave harmony. Because of their magnetic and easygoing personality, they are a favorite with people everywhere. But they also need to put their foot down when needed, as their sacrificing nature keeps getting in the way! For business, life path number, and any agreements requiring peacekeeping abilities, number 2 is a sure shot guarantee of success.

Number 3: This number corresponds to generous spirit, teamwork, and social aspects. They are the life of any party, and people love their witty banter. They also tend to stick with the mundane or shallow pleasures of life instead of learning new things and sticking with something more profound. They are also prone to having more than one romantic relationship. 3s are known for bringing people together and keeping the social fires going.

Number 4: 4s make amazing planners, administrators, organizers, and managers. They have excellent attention to detail and can get along with anyone. They are also adept at getting work from people. When such people wish to date, they must make sure that the other person can keep up with their spirit. Otherwise, it might seem as if the 4 is taking charge everywhere.

Number 5: If your life path number is 5, that means you do not care to be bound to any one thing or person. You are a free spirit and want to do things your way—be it a freelance career or a penchant for travel. You are flexible and open-minded. You need someone similar in thought or the exact opposite to balance out the yin and yang.

Number 6: Sincerity, warmth, and affection are the hallmarks of 6s. These people speak and do things from their hearts. Their natural warmth and love make them a popular choice for careers like teaching, therapy, pediatrician, or social work. When such people make relationships or embark on a new project, they throw themselves completely into it. 6s need to understand that too much of anything might not be that good. They need to learn moderation.

Number 7: Such people have excellent analytical skills and coupled with their intellectual pursuits, it makes them perfectly suited for careers in education, philosophy, detective, or police work. These people work more with their heads, not the heart. Emotions and expressions do not come naturally to them.

Number 8: This number corresponds to hard work, motivation, sincerity, and a sense of purpose. Such people almost always have a great mind for numbers and do well in accounting, finance, and economic advisers. They are methodical and patient. Such people find it easy to make and maintain relationships—although they might find it hard to let go.

Number 9: 9s are all about a humanitarian approach and leadership. They also tend to keep giving until they don't have anything left, but they need to look out for themselves more and stop putting others first.

The Master Numbers

11, 22, and 33 are considered the master numbers in numerology because 1, 2, and 3 form a Triangle of Enlightenment. The other numbers, 44, 55, 66, 77, 88, and 99, are known as Power numbers.

Master Number 11: The most intuitive and analytical of all numbers, 11 corresponds to number 2 in many aspects—insightful, mysterious, deep, emotional, stubborn—but with more leadership and charismatic qualities.

Master Number 22: This is one of the most successful numbers and is also known as "Master Builder." 22 mirrors some qualities of number 11, but it also complements those by its innate nature of 2 and 4—making it more analytical, practical, and idealistic. 22s must learn to be practical; otherwise, they will waste their potential.

Master Number 33: This is the "Master Teacher" and most spiritually and aesthetically sound number. It contains all the qualities of the 11 and 22, along with those of 3 and 6—making it powerful and magnetic! 33 is considered active when found in your life path number, expression number, or personality number. That is when it is most effective.

The Secondary Numbers

Number 10: Indicates the completion of a portion of your life cycle or karmic cycle. Usually considered a good omen.

Number 12: Completing something, rewards, and fortune.

Number 13: Ill luck, sickness, death, bad omens, and restrictions.

Number 14: Mental and physical upheavals, trials, break-in fortune, delays, and curbing of freedom.

Number 16: Intellectual pursuits, emotional coolness, cold attitude toward something or someone.

Number 19: Selfish behavior, laziness, anger, aggression, and powerlessness.

Number 40: Finality in something, the beginning of a new project or relationship.

Now, look at the different aspects of numerology, namely:

1. Life Path Number
2. Year Number
3. Name Number
4. Fate Number
5. House Number

Life Path Number

This is the most important number, which forms the basis of your life and everything you do in it. It reflects who you are, your traits, where you are strong, and where you can improve.

To calculate your life path number, do the following:

Add all the digits in your complete birth date. For example, say Rachel Jones was born on April 6, 1998.

Break it down as:

4+6+1+9+9+8=37

Add 3 and 7. You get 10. Further, add them. You get a single digit 1. This is Rachel Jones's life path number. If your total comes up to 11, 22, or 33, do not add them further. The Master Numbers have different interpretations.

Year Number

Every year brings a different meaning to your life. To calculate your current year number, do the following:

Add the current year to your date of birth. For example, if the current year is 2020, and your date of birth is November 5:

5+1+1+2+0+2+0=11

Your year number is 11.

Name Number

Use the table given below and convert the letters of your name into numbers. Then add them up to get your name number. This reveals your characters and traits.

For example, your name is Rachel Jones.

R=9, A=1, C=3, H=8, E=5, L=3

J=1, O=6, N=5, E=5, S=1

So, Rachel Jones translates as numbers into:

9+1+3+8+5+3+1+6+5+5+1=47

Further, 7+4= 11

So, Rachel Jones gets her name number as 11.

Inner Personality: Add up the vowels in your name.

R A C H E L J O N E S= A, E, O, E

A=1, E=5, O=6

1+5+6+5= 17

1+7= 8

The inner personality number is 8. This is what governs her inner self.

Outer Personality: Add up the consonants in the name.

R A C H E L J O N E S = R, C, H, L, J, N, S

R=9, C=3, H=8, L=3, J=1, N=5, S=1

9+3+8+3+1+5+1= 30

3+0=3

The outer personality number is 3. This is what her public persona is.

Fate Number

To calculate your fate number, add your birth number and name number. If you continue with the above example, you'll see that Rachel Jones has a life path number (birth number) as 1. Her name number is 11.

11 +1= 12

1+2=3

So, Rachel's fate number is 3.

House Number

You simply calculate the numbers in your address. Leave out the street and building names. Reduce it to one single digit. Here are the interpretations:

If your house number is:

1 — Represents self-reliance, quarrels with neighbors, dissatisfaction

2 — Represents harmony and building of good bonds between residents

3 — Represents an outgoing and open-minded nature of people

4 — Represents entrepreneurial spirit, home businesses, life improvement

5 — Represents quiet, energy, activities, and relaxation mode in residents

6 — Represents family, domesticity, and harmony between people

7 — Represents students, introverted nature, stubborn attitude

8 — Represents a need for more money, balance, unexpected arrivals, a bit of strife

9 — Represents intellectual pursuits, music, joy, fortune, new projects

Numbers, just like other aspects of life, have hidden meanings. You can cultivate the wisdom and growth needed to understand and interpret them!

Chapter Six: Palmistry — The Basics of Palm Reading

Reading palms is often a favorite pastime at gatherings or get-togethers. It is mostly fun, but there is a deeper meaning behind all those squiggly lines and bumps on your palm. Palmistry refers to reading hands or palms and assessing someone's personality, future aspects, fortune, etc. This practice is also known as "chiromancy." However, palmistry is just not reading palms; it takes into consideration your fingers, fingernails, and arms too. Every single bit of the palm adds together to bring a whole meaning to a person's character traits and personality.

Palmistry Origins

This ancient practice has its roots in India, Rome, and China. Other countries such as Persia, Greece, and Egypt also use ancient palmistry recordings in their day-to-day lives. Chinese history suggests that palmistry began there almost three thousand years ago. A comprehensive detailing about the practice originated in China during 202 BC–9 AD during the Western Han Dynasty's rule. Xu Fu wrote this treatise.

Aristotle, one of history's greats, elaborated on the practice of palm reading in his book, *De Historia Animalium*, which translates to "*History of Animals.*" He believed that the lines etched in the human hand mean something and are not there without any reason. Now delve into this fascinating ancient practice, which still finds many serious takers today.

Major Palm Lines — What They Are and How to Read Them

If you look closely at your palms, you will see a crisscross of numerous lines. Some may be parallel, intersect, twinning, and yet others might be single. Each line of your hand says something. Time to find out what:

Life Line

This is one of the three major lines in your palm. It begins from the edge of the palm, resting between the thumb and forefinger, and extends toward the thumb base. In general, it tells you about the life energy of the person. The absence of a lifeline is not a good sign. It means you will suffer ill health and possibly have a short life. Frequent accidents are also predicted for such people. In contrast, a deep and long lifeline indicates that the person is highly resistant to ill health and disease and may enjoy a long life.

A thick lifeline may mean that the person is more suited to jobs involving hard physical labor than a desk job. These people will also be good at physical activity and sports. A thin and weak line indicates gynecological problems in females and unsatisfactory career paths in the initial stages of life. A secondary line running parallel with the lifeline means a good, strong vitality for the person involved. He or she may also recover very quickly from illnesses.

Any branches or forks in the lifeline indicate many things: upward branches might mean more opportunities, chances, fame, and prestige in life. Downward branches can mean less energy, so getting diverted from one's goal and loneliness in later years.

Heart Line

This is also known as the "love line" and is of extreme interest to most people! This line usually indicates how a person responds to love and affection. Your personal relationships and how to deal with them become clear with the heart line. A good line is considered deep, unbroken, curved, and extending for a long way without a break. If it has two or more forks at its end, it's all the better!

Length of the Heart Line

Short: A short heart line indicates ruthlessness and narrow-mindedness. Such people act without thinking and, therefore, face problems due to their impulsive nature.

Long: This indicates a certain stubbornness in dealing with people. Career-wise, success is seen, but at a personal cost. In matters of the heart, romance and heartbreak seem to go together. Major troubles can be seen, which are mended with the person's resolve.

Culmination at the Mount of Jupiter

This shows many dreams, love, and great expectations from oneself.

Culmination between the Mount of Jupiter and Saturn.

If the line ends below the forefinger and middle finger, it indicates the purity of one's love.

Curvature

Straight: This indicates a stable, mild, and approachable personality. In romantic overtures, this person is shy and passive. It also indicates a harmonious and stable family life ahead.

Curved: If it is an upward curve, it indicates a lot of eloquence for the person. He or she may be excellent at speaking out and creating a favorable romantic atmosphere. A downward curve, on the other hand, shows a negative temperament. Others might feel uneasy around you due to your inability to show your true self and feelings. Some drama and twists are predicted for this personality's love life.

Islands

Any islands in the heart line indicate changes in your love life, most commonly, emotional and romantic distress. Your love life might experience some sort of breakdown, unwilling attitudes, and other causes for concern.

Broken Lines

If the gap is large, there are indications of a break or hardship in the relationship.

If the line breaks under the little finger, the results indicate stress and hardship in both your material and romantic life. It also indicates an inability to stick or stay faithful to one's partner, thereby causing the relationship to break up.

If the line ends where the ring finger and little finger meet, this sadly indicates a failed relationship or failed marriage. However, all is not lost. It also shows happiness and another true love after the disaster.

If the two broken lines are concurrent, you are more than likely to suffer poor blood circulation and other related ailments.

If none of these and the broken line seems to go on in the direction of its own, it usually means that the person is a bit neurotic, impulsive, and hard to love. This person will most certainly enjoy his or her life the way they want.

Head Line

This line begins from the edge of the palm and extends across it, between the life line and heart line. The head line indicates a person's state of mind, beliefs, the way they think, self-control, etc.

A long head line shows that you have clarity of mind and are considerate and responsive. It would also indicate overthinking.

A medium-length line means that you are smart. You have a talent for doing things in a way that others can't.

A short line extends only up to the middle finger. Such people usually are hasty, impulsive, and careless. Conversely, such people can also be counted upon to finish tasks quickly and creatively.

The Degree of Bending

Straight: This usually indicates that a person is practical and dedicated. He or she is typically an idealist and does well in commerce, science, and math.

Curved: Such people do well in PR, mass media, psychology, and sociology. They have a realistic bent of mind.

Downward: You have a highly creative and artistic ability. Vocations such as painting, murals, poetry, and creative writing will be most suitable for such people. Conversely, people with this kind of line are also quite impulsive when it comes to handling money.

Relation to the Life line

Joined: If joined and then split toward the end, it usually shows the strength of character. If they overlap, it means that the person is shy and thoughtful.

Separated: Such a line depicts an extroverted personality, which is highly independent.

Other Important Lines and Their Interpretations

Marriage Line

One of the aspects usually troubling people is their marital life and status. This line shows your marital situation quite clearly. Some people have a single line, others might have multiple, and yet others might have crossed lines or no lines at all. In the case of a marriage line, the length usually determines the outcome. Of course, apart from that, there are other aspects to interpreting the marriage line too. So, keep reading!

Length

Long and Straight

This is the ideal line, indicating a deep and strong bond of love. A happy and stable family life is interpreted with this line. If this kind of line touches your sun line, the outcome is not only a happy marriage but a successful career path too.

Short

A short line will mean that you are not as passionate about the opposite sex as you should be. If the line does not run deep, it means there is reluctance toward pursuing romantic relationships. Such people also usually marry late in life.

Curvature

Curve Downwards

Ominously, this might mean the death of a partner earlier than your death. A sudden dip in the line might mean an accidental death. A line curving downward and touching the heart line means that you will have clashes and fights with your partner. This is also the line that indicates separation or divorce.

Curve Upwards

A serene love life is the reading for this line. You are stable and happy in your relationship and do not have any financial worries about the future. This kind of line indicates a happy marriage.

Broken Line

A broken line indicates that you will have reservations when it comes to your marital life. Quarrels will be the mainstay of this relationship. If it reaches a certain point, divorce is almost always on the cards.

Crossroads or X sign

In palmistry, anything that has a crossroad or an X sign is considered to be inauspicious because it indicates trouble in paradise. Such people tend to have a greater chance of marital unhappiness and arguments. They may also seek love affairs outside their marriage, which further worsens the situation.

Overlapping Lines

Such lines usually mean that you have a less than ideal relationship. You have ideas and dreams about your mate that are hard to fulfill in reality. If unmarried, you will stay single for a long time. If married, you will find yourself seeking outside pleasures and interests.

Fate Line

The fate line is another major line that runs up the palm near the middle finger's base. It can begin from anywhere. It is also known as the "career line" because this line indicates how well you will do in your chosen career. This line also indicates changes in your work life and career path. If it is clean and deep, you can consider yourself blessed with a great career path and fortune. This line is also referred to as the "line of luck."

Timing of the Fate Line

From the base of the palm, the fate line begins at age five.

The fate line and headline intersect at the point for age 35, and the heart line's intersecting point is for age 55.

If the point for the fate line comes to the Mount of Saturn, it points at age 75.

Absence of a Fate Line

This does not mean that you will not have a fruitful career. It merely means that you tend to keep job-hopping due to your nature and do not wish to maintain any permanency in your career.

The Shape of the Fate Line

Long and Deep

This kind of line usually shows a strong entrepreneurial spirit in the individual. He or she is strongly capable of running their own business.

Narrow and Thin

If this goes from the middle part of the line toward the end of the line, it means that you will have a rewarding career in your early days but get progressively worse during your later years.

Shallow Line

Hard work, albeit with some twists, is indicated for this line. If it is shallow and wide, you will work hard but will fail to reap the benefits of the hard work.

Oblique Line

This shows that the individual has a unique thought process and gives a very refreshing perspective to general ideas and views at work.

Fate Line and the Heart Line

If the heart line stops the line of fate, it usually indicates that your emotions cloud your thinking. You rule with the heart rather than the head. This may affect your career chances.

A fate line that emerges from the Mount of Venus (surrounded by the lifeline at the base of the thumb) and ends near the heart line denotes a marriage with a person of fame and repute.

Fate Line and the Head Line

An early divorce or separation of parents might be the outcome if the head line stops the fate line.

If it merely brushes by the head line and does not penetrate it, it indicates fame and fortune. It also shows that the person does not see a project through. These people would do well to save money from an early age.

If a fate line is stopped at the head line, you stop working of your own free will. Even though you have the talent, a false sense of judgment about your abilities will make you do so. Don't lose heart, though. After age 35, you will have some sort of breakthrough in your work life.

Sun Line

This line begins from the Mount of Moon, which is at the base of the palm on the side of the little finger and goes upward to the Mount of Sun, below the ring finger.

The sun line depicts the kind of talents individuals may possess, their capabilities, and their liabilities. People with a long sun line generally fare better than those without it. A good, strong sun line boosts the fate line.

Some Pointers

If the line is clear, it indicates that the person has a refined taste in literary and artistic pursuits.

If the sun line is short or not present, it indicates an ordinary and placid life. A complete absence would mean a lack of success for the individual.

If the line is thin and narrow, it usually indicates a life of frustration and possible problems in marital life.

Doubled Lines

This shows that the individual is versatile and open to suggestions. This person has varied skills and has a good head for business.

Multiple Lines

If there are more than two sun lines, that means you do not have a head for finance and may lose money. Your expenditure is more than your income. You will need to start saving early and learn a few financial concepts.

Sun Line and Fate Line

If both these lines are parallel in your palm, it is a particularly good sign. This spells success, fortune, and a good reputation for the person throughout their life.

Money Line

The money line can be found under the ring and little finger.

If the line is clear and straight, it indicates that the person is a smart investor and makes smart money decisions. In conjunction with a clear sun line, it could mean that the person will gain both money and fame later in life.

If the money line is wavy, the person's wealth in life will not be stable. There can be troubles in their work or career.

Any other curvature in the line indicates a weathered fortune ahead. If this kind of palm belongs to a generally short-tempered person, it will mean a lot of difficulty in earning wealth and prestige.

Money Line and Sun Line

Sometimes, a sun line branches off and extends toward the little finger, which is also the money line. This kind of line signifies commercial success and a great head for money-related matters.

If the sun line and money line are intertwined or connected, this person enjoys an unexpected windfall later in life.

When a short line crosses the money and sun lines, it would indicate enemies in your life who wish to sabotage you and rob you of your wealth.

M Sign

According to Chinese palmistry, the M sign in a palm is significant. This happens when the career line passes through the head line in an upward formation, and its endpoint touches the heart line, forming an M shape. For individuals having this line, great riches are foretold.

Money Line — Upward Branching

This kind of line means that the person can manage money and handle business or commerce-related aspects. This person would be the go-to for any money-related advice.

Health Line

The most important line for any person! Located at the base of the little finger, it can travel almost anywhere in the palm. It may or may not join any other lines.

There is a slight catch to this line. Although known as the "health" line, its mere appearance on the palm signifies that something is wrong with the bodily systems. Of course, not all health lines are bad. If it is a straight line that does not touch the lifeline, it is considered good. Surprisingly, the absence of a health line is a good sign!

The Shape of the Lines

- *Wavy*: This warns the person of digestive, liver, or gallbladder problems in life. This person might also suffer from gastrointestinal issues.

- *Broken*: Again, the digestive system is at play here. Terraced lines or those with a sharp break spell doom for the GI tract of the individual.

- *Short Lines Cross Over*: This kind of individual may be accident-prone and suffer ill health over a long time.

- *Multiple Short Lines*: This person is usually weak-bodied and sick for a large part of their childhood and adulthood.

Length of the Health Line

Crossing the Head Line

A long health line doesn't necessarily mean good and robust health. In fact, if this crosses the head line, it could mean that one's health might be affected by excessive mental strain.

Reaching Over to the Mount of Venus

If the health line extends to the Mount of Venus, it means there is something wrong with the circulatory system. Such people are more prone to heart and cardiac-related ailments and diseases.

Touching the Life Line

This is usually interpreted to mean an inauspicious sign of health, contrary to the connotation. It indicates a poor circulatory system and a weak heart.

Palm Mounts

Now that you have covered the palm's major lines, it is time to review common mounts in the palm and understand what they mean.

Palm mounts are raised bumps on the flesh of the hand. In Chinese palmistry, there are seven mounts, each named after a different planet and which stand for different characteristics of the individual. These mounts can be found in the following places:

- *The Mount of Jupiter*: Base of the forefinger, above the Mount of Inner Mars.

- *The Mount of Saturn*: Base of the middle finger.

- *The Mount of Apollo*: Base of the ring finger.

- *The Mount of Mercury*: Base of the little finger, above the Mount of Outer Mars.

- *The Mount of Luna or the Moon*: Base of the palm, on the side of the little finger.

• *The Mount of Venus:* Base of the thumb and surrounded by the life line.

• *The Mount of Mars:* Inner Mars is between the mounts of Jupiter and Venus. The Outer Mars is between the mounts of Mercury and Luna. The plain of Mars, a neutral ground, is located in the center of the palm.

Interpretation of the Mounts

The Mount of Jupiter

A well-developed and significant elevation here indicates that the person is career-minded, ambitious, and responsible. This mount displays authority, self-respect, honesty, and reliability in an individual. Such people are naturally predisposed to jobs in the government or with the armed forces. If this mount is underdeveloped, it indicates a lack of honesty, morals, and timidness in the person concerned. This kind of person also shies away from fame and honor. Conversely, if this mount is extra prominent, it means that the person is pretentious, snobbish, and overly ambitious.

The Mount of Saturn

This mount corresponds to perspective and integrity. A well-developed mount in this location shows that you are sincere, independent, and extremely intelligent, more so than average. Such people are good scholars and efficient organizers. If the mount is too depressed and shallow, you might be a lonely person, tending toward superstitions and religious views. On the other hand, if the mount is too high or pronounced, you tend to be a show-off and might not care for others' opinions. If the mount appears to be too large, it means you tend to be more pessimistic than average.

The Mount of Apollo

Apollo translates to beauty, emotions, and wealth. A well-developed mount here signifies a strong affinity toward art and culture. You will be someone who loves the beauty around you. Such people are also compassionate and work for others willingly. A low mount here signifies a lack of interest in the arts.

The Mount of Mercury

This mount represents your ability to think and make decisions in life. A well-developed mount here means that the individual is resourceful and can adapt to any situation in life. Such people do well in emergency services and management-related studies. But the pitfall is a prominent mount—it mounts to bravado and fluff, no substance. If the mount is low, that indicates that the person is negative in predisposition and will not pull together in teamwork.

The Mount of Luna

Much like the Moon, this mount represents mystery, imagination, and many intrigues. If this mount is developed, it signifies a great deal of intuition and imagination and the ability to dream far and wide. Such people are prone to depression, too, because sometimes their sentiments get the better of them. A low mount means the person isn't open to new ideas. A higher mount means the person is highly emotional and open to love and romance. Conversely, if the mount is low, such people do not show any interest in love or commitment. Their lives are rather humdrum.

The Mount of Mars

Inner Mars: Related to an adventurous streak in individuals, a strongly developed mount indicates courage and fearlessness. A mount higher than average could also mean aggression and fighting tendencies. A lower than average mount usually indicates indecisiveness on the part of the person.

Outer Mars: Sometimes also called the Mars Negative, this mount represents self-control. A strong mount here means that you sail through life without any major fears or dangers holding you back. You persevere through setbacks. You are someone who doesn't like taking monetary risks.

Plain of Mars: It is called a plain as it is never too high nor too low. If it's without any crosses or squiggles, it's a good sign. It means clear sailing in life. Any other lines on it indicate that you will have to fight off obstacles to lead a good life.

The Mount of Venus

Much like the Greek Goddess, this mount relates to love and affection. If it is prominent, it shows that the person enjoys companionship and is highly sentimental. If too low, it indicates that the person lacks energy and is coldhearted. If too high, the person becomes overly energetic, which might lead to complications in their love life.

Left vs. Right Hand

Having read this much about the practice and study of palmistry, now look at the difference between the left and right hand.

In palmistry, the left hand is considered to be passive, and the right hand dominant. This applies to most of the population. If your dominant hand is right, you should ideally present that for the reading. If you are left-handed, this hand should be presented for the reading. However, usually, most practitioners read both palms for a better understanding of you.

The Left Hand Reveals: Your wealth position, family, opportunities, potential, personality traits, quirks, and fears.

The Right Hand Reveals: Your action potential, drive, destiny, and future goals.

Reading of both hands is important because both halves make up a full you. You cannot read one and leave the other because that would mean only half a reading. Beware of cheap and pretentious psychics who read only one palm and rattle off predictions. That is not how palmistry works.

Now that you have a basic understanding of the palms' lines and mounts read on to discover yet another delightful and interesting method of divination: the Runes.

Chapter Seven: Runecasting I: How to Cast the Runes

What is Runecasting?

Runecasting is another method of divination that has been around since ancient times. Runes are cast in specific ways, spread, and then interpreted. Now, just like other forms of divination, runes do not give you the exact and literal meaning of your life events. Nothing like "Who am I going to marry?" or "When will I get a promotion?" Like everything else, runecasting is simply a guiding tool. You will find answers here, but do not take them at face value. This method suggests and offers various options and variables to you regarding your issues and problems. You have to look inside yourself and find the answers.

Origin of Runecasting

According to Nordic legend, the Norse god Odin is credited with the discovery of the rune alphabet. Its origins are as deep and ancient as the Norse gods themselves. Runes are alphabets known as the "Futhark." It remained popular in Scandinavian and German countries before spreading out into the outside world. The word "rune" means a mystery or secret. They are mostly made of stone. The runic alphabets are a diverse collection of symbols that represent several meanings. These rune carvings can be found all over the Scandinavian countries. These carvings date back to the Early Bronze age!

The oldest alphabets are known as the "Elder Futhark," which contains twenty-four runes. Over time, this alphabet was modified and transformed into Anglo-Saxon English. A newer version of the runic alphabet is known as the "Younger Futhark." Because of alphabet variations, it seems safe to assume that migration and emigration of people around the world spread the method of runecasting everywhere.

The first six letters of the Elder Futhark literally spell "FUTHARK." Have a look below:

- F for Fehu — wealth, domestic cattle, prosperity, or gain

- U for Uruz — wild ox, determination, or life force

- T for Thurisaz — giant, thorn, problem, force, or unexpected change

- H for Hagalaz — hail

- A for Ansuz — ancestral, one's own god, communication, or knowledge

- R for Raidho — chariot, wagon, vehicle, travel, or movement

- K for Kenaz — torch, beacon, guiding light, fire, or energy

As mentioned earlier, the Runic alphabet evolved to form the English language alphabet. As you might be aware, the word "alphabet" is derived from two Greek words, "alpha" and "beta." The Elder Futhark is the oldest and most recognized alphabet system because it also happens to be the most ancient form of writing, a complete symbolic system, which appeared in Sweden around 400 B.C. Evidence suggests that more than fifty runestones were discovered in the Viking era (950–1100 AD). These stones spread throughout Denmark, Sweden, Greenland, Copenhagen, and Germany.

Cast Runes

You can either buy a set or runes or make your own. In ancient times, runes were made out of a certain wood, but today, there are different types of wood available, such as oak, cedar, or pine. Rune symbols can be carved onto wood, stone, or even painted. Other rune-making materials include metal, bone, pebbles, or crystals. When you are just starting out, a basic and simple set of runes is recommended.

After a while of practicing the craft, you might want to graduate to a special set of runes. See where your inner light guides you, and choose that particular set of runes to be with you on your journey! Like with any other divination method, choosing your rune set and casting with it is a deeply personal choice and should not be influenced by anyone or anything. It is what you do with it that matters, not the material itself. When you get yourself a set of runes, most likely, it will be accompanied by clear and precise instructions. The information tells you what each rune is, what the alphabet means, what the symbols represent, and how you should interpret the meaning by looking at the overall picture instead of focusing only on one symbol or idea.

A Rune Cloth

This is a piece of fabric where you place the runes while doing a reading. Typically, a rune cloth is white and not too big. Do not worry about getting an exquisite and expensive piece of cloth for the runecasting just because you read somewhere that rune casting is a magical and exotic idea. The cloth is only to prevent your rune stones or crystals from becoming dirty. Dust is a deterrent in runecasting and any other reading, so the cloth helps keep the runes clean.

How to Cast Runes

There is no one specified method to do this. However, there are some established patterns and spreads for you to try out.

You need a quiet place and time to begin your reading. Any outside disturbance will cast a shadow on your inner being and add to the turmoil, leading to an inaccurate reading. You need a clear mind to focus on the subject at hand. Take deep breaths and calm your entire body and mind. Think about any issue or question that has been nagging your mind. If you wish, you can say a silent prayer to the god or deity of your choice. Lay your rune cloth in front of you and place the runes upon it.

Just like in tarot, there are several different spreads and layouts for runecasting. But if you are trying this for the first time, go simple. Pick out one rune and analyze it completely. If you get comfortable with a simple spread, you can then try out the other variations.

Before you place the runes on the cloth, move your hand around in the bag and shake them up. This is similar to shuffling the cards in a tarot deck. Like other divination methods, runecasting looks at all influences—past, present, and personality—to come up with a guiding light for the person. In a three-rune cast, you need to pull out three runes from the bag, one at a time, and place them on the cloth. The first of these indicates an overall summation of your situation or issue, the second one deals with the problems you might face in the course of your action, and the third one represents what you should do to overcome these obstacles and sail through to your goal. Another kind of spread is the nine-rune layout.

In Nordic mythology, nine is considered a magical number! For this reading, shuffle your runes and take out nine of them, one by one, and just scatter them on the cloth. There is no set pattern as to where these runes should fall. Now open your eyes and see what pattern has been formed by the runes. Which ones are facing up and down? Are some near the center of the cloth? Some might be toward the far end. See where each rune has fallen and its direction. Then interpret it, keeping in mind your past and present influencers.

How to Interpret Runecasting

As per the Runic alphabet, you will find that each symbol has more than one meaning. Therefore, experts emphasize that you should never simply go by the meaning provided, but instead figure out the overall picture and then make an interpretation. For example, Ehwaz means "horse." It also means "wheel" or "luck." So, does that mean you are getting a horse? Or a new set of wheels? Or maybe you will just get lucky? Could be. However, add that to the other runes and look at the past and present influences and the person's personality. It could mean anything. He or she might have some luck in their travels. Maybe they could gallop in the wind like the horse and find their stable, i.e., their true goal. Sometimes, these three meanings can point to something even better—maybe an unexpected bonus or promotion at work!

Do not worry if you do not get satisfactory results straight away. It takes time, patience, and years of study before you can begin to really understand the runes and their meanings. There are several books and online resources available to guide you in your quest. Please look at them and try your own readings. Of course, as with any other method of divination, you have to rely on your powers of intuition and deduction for a rounded analysis. And just like with tarot cards, an upside-down or sideways rune can have a completely different meaning compared to an upright rune. Make sure you consult your guide to figure out the correct meaning.

How to Take Care of Your Runes

Generally, rune stones or crystals are stored in a small pouch tied with string. The pouch is soft and keeps the runes safely in one place. Alternate means could include a rune box or a rune chest where you can keep your cloth and runes together. Just make sure you clean them after every reading.

Sometimes, blank runes come in a rune set. That could leave ample room for interpretation, but traditional practitioners of the craft have said that they have never encountered anything like a blank rune in their castings. If you wish to remove them from your reading, that is fine too!

Now that you know what runes are and how to cast them look at some layouts and spreads of runecasting in the next chapter.

Chapter Eight: Runecasting II: Layouts and Spreads for Divination

Here are some popular spreads and layouts and their interpretations.

One-rune Layout

The classic and the simplest. You pick one rune out of the bag and lay it on your cloth. This represents your overall attitude and feelings regarding your question.

Two-rune Layout

You pick out two runes and lay them on the cloth. It represents the idea of what was and what could be. The first one could mean aspects of your life, which are unfolding right now, and the second might lead to events in the future and how you feel about them.

Three-rune Layout

This refers to the past, present, and future layout. The first one is the past—things or events that have occurred already, whose influence you are now acting under. The second one is the present, which deals with events currently taking place. The third one is all about the outcome of what you have asked or wished for.

Four Directions Layout

The four directions represent different aspects of your life. The North (Nordri) influences the past, the West (Vestri) the present, the East (Austri) the future, and the South (Sudri) represents all the possible outcomes of this reading.

However, do not interpret this to mean that your future is predicted or that you have a clear look into what will happen. There will be multiple options and outcomes for you, based on how you take the answers.

Five Cross Layout

The first rune represents the question you have asked. The second rune is about all aspects related to the question, which also includes the past. The third rune represents something hidden or overlooked in the question you have asked. The fourth rune tells you about the life forces associated with the question. The fifth rune provides answers or multiple options for the question.

Midgard Serpent Layout

In mythology, this beast was believed to have lived in the ocean and was extremely long. You don't need to place your runes in the same formation, in a flowing curve, as the figure suggests. The figure merely symbolizes a snake; you begin with the tail and slowly advance toward the head. While making this journey, you will climb metaphorical hills and fall into ravines and stumble. There will be periods and patterns of rewards and rest. This is basically life's journey.

The first rune represents your past and your feelings attached to it. The second rune is about what you have undergone concerning particular painful events of the past. This is also related to obstacles and roadblocks. The third rune represents your present—your state of mind and attitude to confront the past and its challenges and overcome present obstacles. The fourth rune tells you to renew your journey. There is a higher hump here, signifying even more problems. The fifth rune gives you a glimpse into your journey. You see your goal and are exhilarated! The sixth one tells you that you need to work hard and put in more effort to reach your goal. The last one represents the snake's head. Symbolically, this is your goal.

Be aware that this does not merely represent a timeline of events for you to reach your goal; it is also a cycle. Once you complete the journey, there is another one waiting for you. This teaches you not to be complacent and placid.

Bifrost Layout

According to Nordic mythology, Bifrost refers to a bridge connecting the world of humans to the world of gods. With this kind of layout, the runes make a deep connection between the material and the astral world.

The layout is like a rainbow, with the VIBGYOR (violet, indigo, blue, green, yellow, orange, and red) colors. Each color means something.

- Red — past attitudes and feelings
- Orange — what you see and perceive in the present
- Yellow — your present attitude
- Green — the effects of your mental state on your present actions
- Blue — what attitude you will hold for the future
- Indigo — the effects of your present attitude on your future
- Violet — the total of your outcome

Grid of Nine Layout

Take the runes out and place them in a grid. The first rune you pick out will go in the middle of the third row, the second rune toward the right corner of the first row, and so on. Adding up the numbers from any of the columns or rows gives you fifteen.

Read the third row first—this is all about your past experiences and feelings about things and people.

The third row contains three runes in order 8, 1, and 6.

- 8 — corresponds to hidden meanings and influences of the past
- 1 — corresponds to basic past instincts
- 6 — corresponds to the present-day attitude and mental state

The second row contains runes in order 3, 5, and 7.

- 3 — corresponds to present influences that are partly obscured
- 5 — corresponds to events that are currently taking place and shaping your life
- 7 — corresponds to your attitude and feelings toward these events

The top row is the last one to be read. It contains runes in order 4, 9, and 2.

- 4 — corresponds to the outcomes of the future, delays, or any roadblocks
- 9 — corresponds to the question at hand and its implications
- 2 — corresponds to what you really feel and think about the problem or question you have asked

Odin's Nine Layout

Historically, this layout represents Odin's body as he hung from a tree. To read this layout, follow these steps:

Think of the layout as having four columns.

The first one has numbers 1 and 2 in it.

- 1 — hidden influences of your past
- 2 — your present attitude to past events

The second column has numbers 3 and 4 in it.

- 3 — the action of obscured influences now

- 4 – your attitude and mental state for events happening currently

The third column has numbers 5 and 6 in it.

- 5 – any obstacles that might prevent you from seeing the outcome
- 6 – your response to the outcome

The last column contains 7, 8, and 9.

- 7 – indicates the powers you already have or will need for the first column
- 8 – indicates the powers you already have or will need for the second column
- 9 – indicates the powers you already have or will need for the third column

The last column, which shows Odin's spear, represents the powers you have or need to deal with each of the previous three columns.

Celtic Cross Spread

This is similar to a tarot layout. In this layout, concentrate on the placement of the first two runes. Ideally, you can have the person casting the runes pick out a specific rune related to their question— love, career, relationships, health, life, etc. If you can, draw a picture depicting this rune and ask the person to concentrate and focus on it during the reading. Another method involves picking out a random rune from the bag and drawing it on the paper. This will be a random one and not necessarily connected to the question the person wants to ask. The second rune should be placed above the first one. However, if not possible, lay it next to the first rune.

- 1 – the issue or question at hand
- 2 – the outside influences that might pose obstacles
- 3 – the hidden influences that affect the issue

- 4 – the personal influences of the person asking the question

- 5 – any fears or misgivings the person has with regards to their question

- 6 – influences from family and friends

- 7 – the dreams and hopes of the person asking the question

- 8 – the anxieties or negative feelings associated with the future

- 9 – the person's handling of their past and present influences

- 10 – the outcome of the entire reading

Egil's Whalebone Layout

This layout is based on a mythological tale in Iceland, telling the story of a poet, Egil, who cures Helga, who fell ill due to incorrectly carved runes. Egil scraped those off and carved healing runes into the stone, which made her better. In this reading, instead of reading each rune individually, they are divided into four groups of three. The interpretation is as follows:

Group 1: Rune Numbers 1, 2, and 3

In the tale, the original carver knew exactly what he was doing. This tells you that when you are looking at the first set of runes, you know what you want from life. You know your intentions, goals, desires, and feelings. You need to keep those in mind as you go ahead.

Group 2: Rune Numbers 4, 5, and 6

Helga, the girl in the tale, falls ill because the carver carved the wrong runes into the stones. This group indicates that if your intentions are wrong or maleficent—if you just see the goal and not the journey leading to it—you might be led astray.

Group 3: Rune Numbers 7, 8, and 9

Helga's father is Thorfinn, and naturally, he was worried about his daughter becoming sick. This group of runes suggests that there will be outside obstacles and thorns in your path. These can be outright roadblocks, or some might come in disguise. Say you need some financial help. You might suddenly receive monetary assistance from someone you never thought would help you. Or, if your goal is to save for the future, your spending habits may not allow you to do so, leading to problems and frustration. The key here is to keep an eye on what you are doing.

Group 4: Runes 10, 11, and 12

Egil, Helga's savior, rubs out the wrong runes and carves healing ones. This rune group tells you to overcome all self-doubt and march toward your goal. Keep all the comments in mind but do not take them to heart.

Now that you have a basic understanding of runes and their meanings, it is time to study another popular divination method: tarot.

Chapter Nine: Tarot Reading I: The Major Arcana

Tarot cards were initially used for fun games during the fifteenth century, but it was only at the beginning of the eighteenth century that they began to be taken more seriously and used in conjunction with divination. Antoine Court and Jean-Baptiste Alliette did some major groundbreaking work to popularize tarot in Paris, from where this all began.

What do You Need for a Reading?

First, you need a deck of cards. There are many different ones to choose from, the most popular being Rider-Waite. Each Tarot card deck has 78 cards divided into two categories, the Major Arcana and Minor Arcana. The twenty-two cards of the Major Arcana refer to major aspects and influences in one's life. The Minor Arcana deals with everyday matters. The 56 cards in the deck are divided into wands, swords, pentacles, and cups. Usually, wands are symbols for creativity, swords for intellectual pursuits, pentacles for money-related matters, and cups for emotional matters. You will read more about the Minor Arcana in the next chapter.

Card Reading — Basics

There are several spreads of the cards. The most common is the "three card spread," the "Celtic Cross," and the "seven day spread." In a three card spread, you shuffle the cards, and the reader pulls three cards from the deck. The first is for the past, the second for the present, and the third for the future. Another common reading is the "daily card reading." A single card is pulled from the deck, and its meaning for the day is interpreted.

Notable Facts About Tarot

- Everyone has a Tarot Birth Card. Want to know how? Add up your birthday! For example, February 10, 1980. That would be 1+0+2+1+9+8+0, which equals 21. 2 and 1 equal 3. That means your Birth Tarot is the Empress!

- The myth that you cannot buy your own tarot card deck, and it has to be gifted, is completely untrue. You can definitely buy your own deck and do a reading.

- Anyone can read the tarot; spirituality is only one aspect of it, but you will need intuition for the reading.

- There are basic elements associated with the tarot. In the Minor Arcana, water is associated with cups, earth with pentacles, air with swords, and fire with wands.

Here are some apps for Android and iOS phones that you might find useful. Try them out sometime!

- Tarot Life and Numerology
- Tarot Card Reading and Astrology
- Astroguide
- Tarot Card Reading
- InstantGo
- Yes or No Tarot

- Free Tarot Reading
- Labyrinthos Tarot
- Trusted Tarot

The twenty-two cards in the Major Arcana of the tarot represent everyday situations, with specific meanings and messages. They are not just cards; they are a storytelling device. The following twenty-two cards represent your life journey and the lessons you learn. Without further ado, it is time to jump into this!

0. The Fool

Upright Position

The first card in the tarot deck, the Fool, is considered a good omen because he is a childlike being, uncorrupted and unaware of life's challenges that lie ahead (just like a child). He is innocent and full of joy and wonder. This card in your reading encourages you to take on the world and its challenges openly. Recognize your potential and act on it.

Reverse Position

If this comes up the other way around, you may encounter another side of yourself, which you haven't explored until now. This part could be hidden in the shadow of ego and ignorance, or you may harbor ill feelings toward someone or have psychological blocks that need to be cleared.

1. The Magician

Upright Position

This card is all about you—your unique nature and skillset that sets you apart from others. If this comes up in your reading, it means you already possess all the skills and tricks needed for you to accomplish your dreams and goals. Nothing is going to hold you back now.

Reverse Position

Conversely, an upside-down card would mean that you are your own worst enemy! You might be unconsciously sabotaging your efforts. Maybe you feel that your thoughts and ideas are too forward and shocking to put into action, or perhaps you are just not aware of what qualities you possess, or you lack the courage to find out.

2. The High Priestess

Upright Position

This might be the most intuitive card of the deck. It deals with your conscious mind, awareness, and also the subconscious. If you get this card, it is telling you to look inside and listen to your inner voice. Your gut already knows what is right and wrong. You just have to trust it and listen to it. In the tarot story, this card appears when the Fool decides to see what kind of powers and skills he can develop.

Reverse Position

This card appears to tell you that you are so immersed inside your life, thoughts, and ideas that it has now become an unhealthy obsession. There is another world outside that needs equal exploration. This card tries to teach one about balance.

3. The Empress

Upright Position

The most feminine card in the deck, this card in a reading depicts love, beauty, and tenderness. It also denotes fertility and Mother Nature. The Empress is also called "The Great Recycler" because she can reanimate and restore any havoc and upheavals, which distort and destroy your peace.

Reverse Position

If seen in reverse, this card represents nature—unleashing storms, tsunamis, and hurricanes, symbolically speaking. It suggests a surge in repressed emotions that may trigger untold misery if not checked early.

4. The Emperor

Upright Position

This card denotes power, ambition, and leadership. The Emperor is a force to reckon with, as he has weathered many a battle. He also represents authority, structure, and solidity in his being.

Reverse Position

If you get a reverse card of the Emperor, it usually denotes a tendency of being bossy, argumentative, and behaving like a tyrant. You might love being flattered and praised a lot for your good work. This is not a good sign in the long run. You may lose friends and only end up with sycophants for company.

5. The Hierophant

Upright Position

He is a heavenly messenger. His job is to bring spirituality and mystic lessons to people on Earth. This particular card in a reading means that you need to understand and follow the rules. You are also encouraged to find some spiritual outlook.

Reverse Position

This indicates rebellion from your side. However, be aware that the very tradition against which you are rebelling also serves as a soothing and calming influence at times.

6. The Lovers

Upright Position

If this card comes up in your reading, it usually means that relationships in your life and love life need some attention. Apart from love, this card can also mean a crossroads in your life, where you need to assess all choices before making a decision.

Reverse Position

This means that you are facing resistance, or maybe someone is opposing your relationships. You may also have vested interests in the opposition. You have to come clean to yourself if you want to come out of this situation.

7. The Chariot

Upright Position

This card denotes determination and a drive to succeed. It lets the person know that, along with determination, a powerful mind and thought process can make them successful and happy.

Reverse Position

If the Chariot is reversed, it could mean that you need to take charge of certain aspects of your life and bring them up to level with the rest of your personality or life events. You may also need to address your inner resistance to change and overcome it.

8. Strength

Upright Position

This card is not just about physical strength; it is also about your mental strength and aptitude, your heart's courage, and your ability to take life on its own terms. If this card arrives in your reading, it denotes that you are willing to face life on your terms and are ready for everything.

Reverse Position

Conversely, this card may mean that you do not have the power of persuasion. You will need to work hard to overcome the out-of-control and wild mental tendencies you have to succeed.

9. The Hermit

Upright Position

A hermit wants to be alone. This card signifies that you wish to withdraw from the outside world's noise and chaos and seek meaning within. The only challenge here is recognizing a teacher when you see one—as the teacher may be silent, invisible, or speak in a different tongue.

Reverse Position

This could mean a fear of being alone or a resistance you feel before going down the path of wisdom because you fear the awesome power of your intellect.

10. The Wheel of Fortune

Upright Position

This wheel is revolving like an actual wheel. The appearance of this card means that nothing in life is permanent. Everything is cyclical—good, bad, love, hate, riches, and poverty. Everyone has to go through these stages. The only constant thing is change.

Reverse Position

Reversal of fortune is usually depicted in this card. This means you need to go back and start from the beginning. Remember, this is good because the only way from rock bottom is up!

11. Justice

Upright Position

There is an equal and opposite reaction to each karma that you do in life. Life gives you right now what you did in your past—whether it is a punishment or reward. In other words, what goes around, comes around. If this card is in your reading, you need to take stock of your actions and check whether you are doing things right or not.

Reverse Position

A reversed card won't immediately be clear to you because sometimes, there are reasons beyond your capacity to understand. You will need to have patience and wait for the truth to be revealed to you.

12. The Hanged Man

Upright Position

This card reveals a limbo position you might be in. You are confused about something and cannot decide where to make a move. It might also indicate a lack of stability in your personality and lesser energy.

Reverse Position

This could mean that you wish to sacrifice your happiness and want something for someone else's greater good. With no apparent benefit to you, this is almost a selfless act of altruism!

13. Death

Upright Position

Perhaps the most misunderstood card ever, death does not mean an inauspicious card at all. It means a new beginning! It represents the ending of a project, plan, or relationship and hints toward a new one.

Reverse Position

Conversely, this might imply that you have held onto something for a long time and fear letting it go. You fear the consequences or the future and do not wish to change your regular patterns.

14. Temperance

Upright Position

A card like this means moderation, patience, and peace. If this appears in your reading, it means you are on the right path in that particular aspect of your life, and you should definitely go with the flow.

Reverse Position

But beware! If this card is reversed, it could mean that you are tired of yourself and wish to give up. There is a lot of apathy and self-neglect too. You only look at the negativity and chaos in your life and find it difficult to enjoy the sunny spots in your life.

15. The Devil

Upright Position

Ah, speak of the Devil, and he appears! This card indicates certain overpowering feelings of powerlessness in your being. You feel as though you are stuck in a particular situation in your life, and there is no hope. Your internal compass surges on the negativity of the situation.

Reverse Position

On the contrary, if this card appears in the reverse position, you could be a troublemaker! You usually enjoy being in the thick of things and may even be the cause of chaos. This card tells you to monitor your behavior.

16. The Tower

Upright Position

This card is feared for a good reason because it represents the destruction of something that you love. However, keep in mind that a weak structure cannot withstand life's forces. Something has to crumble for something else to rise in its place.

Reverse Position

Breathe a sigh of relief! The worst is over. This card indicates the upheaval in your life is drawing to a close and new beginnings are around the corner.

17. The Star

Upright Position

Just like stars in the night sky, this card signifies hope, calm, and healing. This is a sure sign that the universe is working with you and wants you to succeed.

Reverse Position

It could mean that you are diverted from your own nature, goals, and skills. You may feel alienated from yourself at times. This is the time to refocus on your talents and gifts and put them to good use.

18. The Moon

Upright Position

This card appears if you are feeling anxious, fearful about something, tense, and unusually miserable. It is also connected to your soul and subconscious mind. It tries to tell you the state of your inner being.

Reverse Position

This card indicates that you might be lying to yourself or trying to delude yourself in some way, which does not hurt your ego and keeps it safe. There is a strong temptation to be swept away, but you have to exercise control before it overpowers you.

19. The Sun

Upright Position

Just like the bright and cheerful sun in the sky, this card embodies happiness, vitality, and pure freedom. If this card comes up, rest assured that things are going well for you.

Reverse Position

This implies that you need to be humble and grateful for all the blessings and successes coming your way.

20. Judgment

Upright Position

A crucial card; this is where the past, present, and future are tied together. As with a real judgment, here you are reminded that your present actions will determine your future. It is also known as the Resurrected card.

Reverse Position

This usually means that there is something external that keeps blocking your success. You need to face these restrictions head-on if you want any chance of happiness.

21. The World

Upright Position

If this card comes up in the reading, it means you are exactly where you are meant to be in life. Be it your career, life, marriage, love, health—you have arrived at that particular aspect. This is like your ultimate realization.

Reverse Position

This is a slight bump in the road for you, nothing serious. You just need to meet these minor obstacles with a smile and get on with your life.

Had fun with the Major Arcana? It is now time to dive into the even wider pool of the Minor Arcana cards!

Chapter Ten: Tarot Reading II: The Minor Arcana

You learned what the Major Arcana cards mean in the previous chapter. Now, you will read about the Minor Arcana cards, which means "minor secrets." Therefore, this aspect deals with things and ideas that fall under the day-to-day realm, small-scale projects, minor issues, etc. However, just because these cards do not deal with the personality at large does not mean they are any less important than the Major Arcana cards. Little details make up entire beings, and so, these cards are equally important to people.

There are 56 cards in the Minor Arcana, which can be categorized as follows:

- Suit of Wands (fourteen cards)
- Suit of Pentacles (fourteen cards)
- Suit of Cups (fourteen cards)
- Suit of Swords (fourteen cards)

Each of these is similar to a regular deck of cards, beginning with the Ace, continuing until 10, and then the four special cards: Page, Knight, Queen, and King. Now it is time to dive into the study and interpretation of the Minor Arcana cards.

Suit of Wands

This card is associated mostly with the fire element and the solar plexus chakra. It relates closely to those passions and dreams that you want to accomplish with great fervor and intensity. Whether you make plans and stick to them or give up easily in the face of obstacles is what these suits of cards show you. Wand cards show where you lack: balance in life, the confidence to tackle issues, leadership skills, and inner strength. Each of the cards holds the power to change the reading instantly—from positive to negative and vice versa.

Ace of Wands

Upright Position

This usually denotes a step of immediate consequences that might lead you toward or away from your goal. It indicates a new beginning in life or endeavor and also whether you possess the necessary drive to complete the project. It shows that you are now ready to take a new step forward—either in your career, relationship, or any other important aspect of your life.

Reverse Position

This can mean that you do not like change and resist it actively. But it also prods you to understand this scenario and gives you the courage to overcome the odds.

Two of Wands

Upright Position

This is the second step in your life's journey. This card signifies that you need to come out of your comfort zone and take on something new. A decision also needs to be made. Sometimes, it also indicates that you are at a crossroads or dead end in your life. When this comes up in your reading, it means that you need to assess all your options carefully before going ahead. If you don't, it can mean many regrets later on. You need to understand all the implications of your decision or action before taking a step forward.

Reverse Position

This indicates that you are stuck momentarily in deciding something, and you need a slight nudge in the right direction to steer you toward your goal.

Three of Wands

Upright Position

This card indicates that you already have an inner balance, which lets you test the waters before putting your toes in. This also signifies that you are capable of taking calculated risks and accomplish lofty goals. In a reading, this card urges you to look around and keep your eyes open for opportunities and chances, which you would typically miss.

Reverse Position

On the other hand, this card also indicates a temporary lack of willpower in some people. You might have already reached the burnout stage.

Four of Wands

Upright Position

This card usually means teamwork. It indicates the laying of a cornerstone, in harmony and together with other people. It denotes a home renovation activity, marriage, relationship, big project, etc. Start-up companies and entrepreneurial ventures are suggested when this card is revealed in your reading.

Reverse Position

A reverse position in this card means that you need to brush up on your people skills, team-building skills, and problem-solving skills. You need to actively work on it because not doing so will cause problems in your projects and life.

Five of Wands

Upright Position

This card signifies ambition, competition, and even aggression—to some extent. When this card appears in your reading, it means you should ask yourself some tough questions: *Why are you fighting this particular battle? Against whom? What do you expect to gain from it?* If your answer is: "Personal gain and making others feel low," you need to check your priorities. Winning is not everything in life.

Reverse Position

In reverse, this card points out that you are egotistical and cannot form friendly bonds with others. You have great difficulty being a team player. When this happens, you need to ask yourself: "What can I do to make this situation better? How can I make others feel comfortable around me?"

Six of Wands

Upright Position

This represents recognition and acknowledgment for your earnest effort. If you think of a victory parade or joyous celebration, that is the card's picturization! It is a message from above that's encouraging you to believe in yourself, not give up, act with grace and dignity, and accept the praise that comes your way. This is also a card that denotes celebrations and relaxation.

Reverse Position

You might be uncomfortable taking on a leadership role in the community, but this card denotes that you should—because of the great learning experience!

Seven of Wands

Upright Position

If this card comes up in your reading, it means that you will most likely be successful in all of your endeavors. You will be recognized for your talents and accomplishments. However, you also need to beware of the pitfalls of fame. You cannot afford to be smug and proud about this. By all means, enjoy your success, but do not let the ugly head of conceit devour you.

Reverse Position

This card indicates a lack of motivation, self-esteem, and pressure. You might need to figure out why you are resisting the very same factors that will make you successful. Being honest with yourself will help. Find out what is holding you back and fight it.

Eight of Wands

Upright Position

Events and things in your life are moving at a quick speed now. This card indicates change and that change is necessary for the evolution of human beings. Things do seem out of control but do not waste your time and energy trying to pin it down. Go along with the change, and you may be surprised at the new turn your life takes!

Reverse Position

With this card in your reading, it usually means there are a lot of changes ahead for you in your life. You cannot assume that everything is fine and dandy and carry on in the usual manner. You need to accept and acknowledge these changes if you want to achieve your goals. Otherwise, you'll be stuck in a rut.

Nine of Wands

Upright Position

This depicts the need for rest, recuperation, and restoration of your energy. Step back and let others be the hero for a change. They are just as capable as you are to fight challenges and rise to the occasion. Let them be in the spotlight for a while. Help others who need you right now. If you see this card, it depicts someone who is too exhausted to work but, at the same time, too proud to ask for help. Do not be this person; instead, let others help you out for a change.

You need to seek new perspectives on something that is bothering you or something you have been working on, or even a totally different point of view in life. Be true to yourself.

Ten of Wands

Upright Position

In contrast, this card is all about energy and action. There is no time to relax! You have to plow on and see the project or event until its very end. Even if this means giving up what you love doing, you have to complete your task. Wisely, this card reminds you to take up only one thing at a time—multitasking is not indicated here because this card represents a total and undying commitment.

Reverse Position

This indicates that perhaps you have lost your sense of direction and perspective in life. You aren't objective enough to see where you are going wrong. When this card appears, you need to take a step back and reevaluate. Remember why you are doing what you're doing. This might give you a clearer perspective.

Page of Wands

Upright Position

This indicates someone who is a non-conformist and an independent and solitary individual by nature. He or she is an innovator or a rebel. This card indicates freedom, power, passion, and development. This is an exciting card because it denotes the interests and passions of the person involved. Even though the person may appear to be simple, they possess the qualities to become a great leader.

Reverse Position

You may be concerned about what your image is like in society. You always put your best foot forward in public and worry about it in private.

Knight of Wands

Upright Position

This is a feisty person who is easily provoked. This card in your reading reminds you to keep a check on your temper and attitude. Sure, you can be intense, but make sure that this intensity does not get the better of you!

Reverse Position

This indicates that the person seeks some change and transformation within themselves or the situation around them. Others may not take too kindly to this, but instead of flying off in a rage, it would be better to understand their points of view too.

Queen of Wands

Upright Position

This person is a born leader who works well with people and sees to it that everyone is cohesive and works together. Their energy is infectious and all-consuming! This person gets things done by using the magic of people working together harmoniously. Such people make excellent managers because they know exactly what their team members are capable of, and they give them wings to fly. Another side of this person is that you can gain no sympathy from them. If they ascertain that your role is over and you can no longer be productive in that setting, they will let you go without hesitation.

Reverse Position

If this card comes up in a reading, it indicates that the person might be bossy and controlling. Others around them may not take too kindly to this kind of persona and may rebel, causing even more damage. The learning here is to trust other teammates and give them confidence.

King of Wands

Upright Position

This card indicates that you wish to lead, are ambitious to a fault, and are practical. You are the center of attention, and you love to surround yourself with your loved ones and lavish love on them.

Reverse Position

This card indicates an imminent danger in you becoming proud. You may undermine others' authority and try to stake a claim in every aspect. Not everyone likes this kind of domination. You should learn to curb such tendencies and nip them in the bud.

Suit of Cups

These cards indicate the state of your emotions, relationships, and how intuitive you are with the people around you. They deal with guidance in love and romance, friendship, and other partnerships.

Ace of Cups

Upright Position

This shows a hand with a cup containing an endless supply of fluid. It signifies your open heart, overflowing with love and concern for others. This indicates the healing and soothing areas of your life.

Reverse Position

Conversely, this could mean a loss of optimism in you or a lack of self-esteem. When this happens, reflect on what is making you feel that way. It might be external or internal factors. Try to make fewer moves here until you are sure of what you are doing.

Two of Cups

Upright Position

This usually means bonding, union, soul mates, partnership, romance, etc. This card indicates a karmic connection between people, a deep understanding. You need to focus on your relationships and make them work.

Reverse Position

This means that perhaps you are putting too much time and effort into your relationships. Your sense of identity and importance comes from external factors. You should stop that and instead work on internal validation.

Three of Cups

Upright Position

This denotes some sort of agreement, teamwork, and bonding with others in your life. It indicates that you are surrounded by like-minded people who are working toward a common goal. You need to acknowledge and appreciate these people in your life. Reconnect and stabilize with them.

Reverse Position

This might imply a lack of trust and understanding on your part for the people in your life. You may feel left out and out of place or out of sync. Try and communicate with them and clear out any misunderstandings.

Four of Cups

Upright Position

This is quite a dispirited and restless time in your life. You may be dissatisfied with something, want a change, or are feeling stagnant. However, this card also tells you to be aware that you may lose out on the simple joys of life that are right in front of you in your reckless abandon. You need to be open and willing to let new things and events enter your life.

Reverse Position

This may manifest as passive aggression on your part. You need to recognize the symptoms and try to wean yourself from them.

Five of Cups

Upright Position

Emotional disturbance, grief, upheavals, messes, expectations, etc., are indicated by this card. You may be disappointed with an outcome or sad over the loss of something. The only way forward is to forgive, forget, and heal from within.

Reverse Position

In an interesting combination of factors, this card indicates that what you perceive to be the worst thing to happen to you might be a blessing in disguise! If you have any phobias, fears, negative experiences, expectations, etc., this card helps you understand and deal with them.

Six of Cups

Upright Position

This card indicates openness, innocence, learning, and optimism. This takes you right back to your childhood. This card tells you to be open and carefree like a child and enjoy fresh experiences with a fresh mind.

Reverse Position

You have a wonderful chance to let past things, events, and hurts go and look forward to a new chapter in life. Revisiting old wounds will be easier because you now know how to deal with them.

Seven of Cups

Upright Position

This card deals with imagination. You dislike your present life and imagine another life where all your dreams may have come true. Though this card indicates that you can change your destiny, it also warns you not to lose sight of reality.

Reverse Position

Your lack of purpose in life has given rise to problems like lack of curiosity, joy, ability to dream, etc. This card encourages you to get all that back. Do not dwell on your current state of mind but work toward getting your mojo back!

Eight of Cups

Upright Position

This indicates betrayal, heartache, and emotional disappointment. This card in a reading is a message for you to walk away from anything that does not seem to be working, even after many trials.

Reverse Position

An event has set you back or hurt you perhaps, but you refuse to let it affect your life. Your resilience and cool attitude will definitely help you out of this spot.

Nine of Cups

Upright Position

A happy card signifies fulfillment and contentment. This is also known as the "Wish Card." You know things will get better if you get this card in a reading.

Reverse Position

Surprisingly, this means that you get what you thought was right for you, but ultimately that is not the case at all. It usually signifies that your dream isn't making you feel as happy as it should, and maybe it is time to set a new goal.

Ten of Cups

Upright Position

This is one of the most joyous cards you can ever get because it signifies togetherness, family, and celebrations!

Reverse Position

Conversely, this card indicates that harmony and togetherness in a group or family are decreasing slowly. There are judgment and criticism. The only way out is through communication and meditation.

Page of Cups

Upright Position

This indicates a very imaginative, idealistic, open, young, mystic, and sensitive person. If this turns up in your reading, you may be at the beginning of a relationship or something new at work.

Reverse Position

This suggests those around you have been indulging you for some time, even though they don't have to. Try not to force yourself on them, and make sure to reach out to them, communicate, and give their needs some consideration.

Knight of Cups

Upright Position

This person is profoundly educated, charming, and a smooth talker. There is a lesson here to balance your inner and outer world, your dreams and realities, and practical aspects and thoughts. Great emotional fulfillment is indicated here.

Reverse Position

This person keeps making excuses and blaming others for things going wrong in their life. It's a message to take responsibility for your actions. This card also offers up a major life lesson this way.

Queen of Cups

Upright Position

This person is well balanced, intuitive, and stable. He or she relates to others at a deep level. This card reminds you to trust your inner self.

Reverse Position

This card indicates that you block your pain by not dealing with it. That is not the answer. You need to be honest with yourself and work through the pain. That is the only way to heal.

King of Cups

Upright Position

This person is balanced, intense, and intuitive. This card suggests that you dig deep inside yourself to figure out the how and why of your relationships with people.

Reverse Position

This card indicates that you might be sour toward someone or hold a grudge. Learn to admit the wrongs and the hurt caused by the person and forgive them.

The Suit of Swords

These cards depict challenges, conflicts, and how you overcome them. They correspond with the Air element. They have a deep connection with truth and reason and, therefore, are associated with fairness and justice.

Ace of Swords

Upright Position

This represents your vision in life, optimism, guiding light, and hope. If it turns up, that means you are beginning something new. You need some clarity to go on with the task.

It could mean that you are obscuring your vision and not seeing the matter at hand clearly. That could be due to your illusions or biases. You need to reexamine your perspective before moving on.

Two of Swords

Upright Position

This indicates that you have two conflicting ideas that you need to examine before you decide on something. You are unsure about what path to take.

Reverse Position

This card could mean that while you can definitely move forward, sometimes, it is better to consult with other people before deciding on something. Take more input and feedback.

Three of Swords

Upright Position

You might know this card very well. It represents sorrow, unhappiness, or separation. It usually indicates that sad times are coming, or you might already be grieving over something. But though painful and sad, this card also teaches you about experiencing pain, going through it, and coming out stronger.

Reverse Position

This suggests that some of the sadness in your life could be dissipating, and there is mending on the horizon. Conflict resolution seems to be the mainstay of this card.

Four of Swords

Upright Position

If this card turns up in your reading, it means you need to take some time out for yourself, maybe retreat into a safe and relaxed place for a while. If not, you will suffer burnout. You need this rest.

Reverse Position

If you have been single, lonely, and solitary for a long time, it is now time to enter the social world. You should balance both solitude and interpersonal relationships. This card teaches you about being in a socially and emotionally balanced state.

Five of Swords

Upright Position

This card represents tension, conflict, aggression, anxiety, and loss. You need to evaluate what kind of battles you are fighting in your life, against whom and how wise or unwise they are. You definitely need to think before you spring into action.

Reverse Position

You are beginning to take success and failure in your stride. You gain some control over your aggression, and you have also learned to take criticism with a pinch of salt.

Six of Swords

Upright Position

This is a tricky card. If you get this in a reading, it could mean that you are attempting to walk away from a difficult situation, which, on the one hand, feels burdensome, but you're also afraid to walk away from it. Maybe you fear what lies ahead but trust yourself and go anyway. You will reap the rewards later.

Reverse Position

This card urges you to put your brain to its fullest use—logic, thinking, reasoning, and analysis; everything has to be used by you. You are somehow not doing so, resulting in apathy and limitations in your ability.

Seven of Swords

Upright Position

This card indicates betrayal and deception. There may be someone in your life that isn't whom they seem to be. Beware of such people. This card also tells you that it is better to be a smart worker than a hard worker. Not only will you save time, but you will also learn new skills in the process.

Reverse Position

This card suggests that there will be setbacks in your life, despite your dedicated efforts. The lesson is not to let that get in your way or blame yourself.

Eight of Swords

Upright Position

When you see this card in your reading, it means that you are stuck somewhere, maybe bound to something. You may have also trapped yourself in your limitations and assumptions. You have to break free by opening your mind and self to new possibilities.

Reverse Position

You tend to blame others for your problems, or you rationalize your defeat in some way, rather than taking accountability for yourself. You need to face your inner self and be honest here if you wish to make any progress.

Nine of Swords

Upright Position

This card indicates loss of control, anxiety, and fears. But look at it closely, as all this stress is self-caused. You need to work through the worry and stress by eliminating negative thinking.

Reverse Position

This usually signifies a chance to banish negativity and depression from your life. You are now ready to embrace the light and leave the darkness behind.

Ten of Swords

Upright Position

This card is all about finality and limits. When this card comes up in a reading, it means that whatever you were working on or a relationship you were holding onto has now reached its natural end, and it's time to let go.

Reverse Position

You need a reality check at this point. Maybe you have begun justifying and dramatizing your problems and fallacies to gain sympathy. You need to snap out of the dream state and accept responsibility for your actions.

Page of Swords

Upright Position

This card in your reading urges you to slow down and take a look at facts before rushing off to implement your plans. Enthusiasm is great, but misinformed enthusiasm will present trouble. You should also beware of people with an ulterior motive.

Reverse Position

You tend to lecture others about their faults, or you may be very prejudiced. You need to curb some of your critical tendencies if you wish to work with others.

Knight of Swords

Upright Position

This card indicates a "bursting to go" quality. However, you need to ask yourself where exactly you are going, your intentions, and how you will treat your success and failure. There is a danger here of jumping to conclusions and not thinking before acting.

Reverse Position

A slightly unfortunate card, this suggests that you may avoid conflict altogether by sweet-talking your way out of tight spots. You may also overpromise and under deliver and make promises you can't keep. Come out of these situations by being honest with yourself.

Queen of Swords

Upright Position

This person is honest, wise, independent, and generally self-aware. It is a message to stand up for and fight for yourself and your rights. Do not let anything and anyone brainwash you into something you are not.

Reverse Position

You might not acknowledge your deepest feelings about something or someone. But you do need to accept them if you want to avoid isolation. Bring your natural compassion out by being open and helping loved ones.

King of Swords

Upright Position

This card indicates truth, happiness, intelligence, candor, and wisdom. You may find yourself in a position in life where others look up to you for guidance and truth. You are powerful and supremely content with yourself.

Alas, this card offers up a suggestion that you are impervious to conscience and integrity. Something less noble has taken their place. Fight with yourself to awaken your inner goodness before it becomes too late.

The Suit of Pentacles

These cards are related to work, career, money, health, and family. They are used mostly to answer questions about these aspects and to learn more about your personality and connections with each of these elements. Pentacles are also referred to as "coins," so do not get confused if you read "coins" instead of pentacles in the interpretations below.

Ace of Pentacles

Upright Position

This represents the first step you put toward your goal, support provided to you, and fulfillment. It has a deep connection with the earth. It tells you that if you hone and polish your talents and craft, you can grow exponentially. The card suggests winning and control over your emotions.

Reverse Position

You need to reconnect with yourself and the values you prize. You have to look within yourself to understand what drives you. If not, success won't come to you easily.

Two of Pentacles

Upright Position

This is usually depicted by a juggling figure where two pentacles swoosh around the figure, unclear where to go. If this card comes up in your reading, it means that there are some changes about to happen in your life, and you need to have the patience to see and understand what they are. Until you do so, you will always be in a tizzy.

Reverse Position

You may have to let go of certain thought patterns. For instance, you may be too polar about an issue where you actually might benefit from being neutral. However, yes, when it concerns helping others, you have to take charge and be proactive.

Three of Pentacles

Upright Position

This can be called the card of the genius. More often, this indicates a master at work, creativity, and fulfillment. Stay focused on your task at hand and see it through. It also indicates collaboration and improvement in the task.

Reverse Position

You may be afraid of sharing your gifts and talents with the outside world, fearful of the comments and reactions of others. Maybe you think it is not worth doing all that. Please keep in mind that only a few people are ever given the gift of being a genius. Try and spread the divine inspiration around.

Four of Pentacles

Upright Position

This is the card of the classic catch-22. You have material comforts and are fully secure, but with that comes the dreaded responsibilities. In your reading, this card is a message to make a rational judgment and not waste your wealth—spiritual or material. You may be holding on tightly to something. Perhaps it's time to let it go and discover what contentment really means.

Reverse Position

This card indicates that you let resentment and an overbearing attitude get in the way of reaching your goals. You may be worried about something, or a task does not go well according to your standards. But that is mainly due to your attitude. Change it, and the world changes!

Five of Pentacles

Upright Position

This card suggests that you should think before setting your goals, especially those that involve short-term or temporary gains. You will definitely feel resentment and anger if your short-term goals aren't met. This card is a reminder that apart from money, there are other untold riches around you. Don't let money run your life. There's more to it than you know.

Reverse Position

This indicates that perhaps you need to be more honest with yourself. You are deceiving yourself or trying to hide from your truth. Instead of daydreaming about potential gains and riches, you need to look at yourself and figure out what you want.

Six of Pentacles

Upright Position

This card is all about giving and receiving generous spirit, knowledge, and support to others. When this card appears in your reading, this is the time for you to give rather than receive. You need to pay the kindness back, pay generosity back, and help someone else. This maintains the karmic cycle of checks and balances.

Reverse Position

Conversely, it could come to mean that you are focused on the idea of getting things back—both literally and figuratively. Your idea of payback is now all-consuming. This has become more important to you than actual giving, which may affect your karma too.

Seven of Pentacles

Upright Position

Traditionally, this card means "to cultivate something." When this card comes up in your reading, it tells you that you need to be extra vigilant with your life—projects, career, home, relationships, or family—to reach your goal. You cannot harbor any excuses. Keep your head down and race toward the finish line.

Reverse Position

This suggests that you like taking risks and gambling with your life. You have somehow lost your direction and way in the world and are willing to risk everything you have for another stab at a chance. Beware of such actions. Do not attempt anything rash at this point.

Eight of Pentacles

Upright Position

This card encourages you to expend more energy, get a fresh perspective on life, and create a balance. This card is about working hard and trying out new ways to improve one's self. Yes, there is a temptation to become a workaholic, which you must curb. You will begin to think of yourself as indispensable, whereas the reality is quite different. Strike a balance.

Reverse Position

Your work begins to take on a large part of your identity and spills into every other aspect of your life. This isn't healthy, and you need to make time for other aspects as well. Work is work, not life.

Nine of Pentacles

Upright Position

This card carries a message that you need to slow down and see if you are just working too hard and not balancing it with other life aspects. This card indicates money, financial stability, and independence. It's important to balance your monetary needs with other desires in life.

Reverse Position

You are possibly in indulgence mode. You feel lethargic and apathetic to your life situation and events. This card indicates that a boost of external energy is coming your way to spur you in the right direction!

Ten of Pentacles

Upright Position

This represents the amalgamation of a lot of effort for achieving your goals—be it a house, car, new promotion, or more money. This card also represents happy and close families, knowledge, comforts, and long-term thinking.

Reverse Position

You may have to start over from scratch after having experienced losses in certain areas of life. While it may seem tedious, starting over can be a blessing too!

Page of Pentacles

Upright Position

This card indicates someone who wants to learn, experiment, do research, learn from their mistakes, grow from experiences, and learn how to deal with failure. Quite an important card!

Reverse Position

This suggests that maybe you doubt your skills and talents. You are unsure whether you can be of service to society. It can also mean that you do not like being social to this extent—but give it a try as it won't hurt anything. You can cultivate more discipline that way.

Knight of Pentacles

Upright Position

This card comes with a message that you need to be patient, methodical, dedicated, and persevere with your efforts. This is the most peaceful card in the entire deck. You have to see the bigger picture and ignore the small fallacies in your path. Sure, the work may not always be up to your standard, but there are dignity and grace in all types of work. Rewards will surely follow.

Reverse Position

In life, you will encounter certain people who do not appreciate you or your worth. This card tells you just to ignore those people. Instead, focus your energy and time on those who love and appreciate you.

Queen of Pentacles

Upright Position

This card indicates healing, education, problem solving, encouragement, and compassion. If this comes up in a reading, it means that you need to take care of yourself and work toward giving yourself and your loved ones a comfortable and nurturing environment.

Reverse Position

It is a warning against becoming too attached to something or someone. You may have been addicted to something or someone in your life, with a negative outcome. This card tells you to break free of this habit.

King of Pentacles

Upright Position

This card is all about accomplishments, financial power, respect, and strength. This card also represents the attainment of your long-term goals. If this comes up in your reading, the message is to work even more methodically so that your gains are higher. Not just in material terms, but spiritual gains too.

Reverse Position

This suggests that perhaps, over time, you have become rather self-centric. Now is the time to switch back to self-discipline and control your desires and mold your abilities. Do not bite off more than you can chew.

In this chapter and the previous one, you have learned all the Major and Minor Arcana cards from the Tarot. In the next chapter, you will study the types of card spreads and how to read and interpret them.

Chapter Eleven: Tarot Reading III: Spreads and Layouts

Now that you have a fair understanding of the Major and Minor Arcana cards, you can begin your own reading. You can buy a set of cards or maybe have someone gift them to you!

Before you dive into a reading, it is important to ask yourself, "Why am I asking the tarot this question?" You need to figure out your real intentions first because the universe knows everything. You cannot bluff it. A simple "yes" and "no" type of question-answer might be useful for beginners, but it will not answer the deepest desires of your heart. For yes/no questions, you might be better off with a pendulum.

Tarot cards are specifically designed. Each card contains its own interpretation, and when combined with other cards, they reveal a wealth of information and guidance for you to follow. Take advantage of this inherent nature of the cards and ask deep and insightful questions.

Here are some of the most popular tarot spreads and layouts for you to choose and try.

The One Card Spread

The most basic reading of all, this layout is as important as the others and is usually favored by beginners. For this reading, you need to shuffle your deck and pick out a card. It represents a question you have in mind and have been wanting to find the answer to for a long time. For more clarity, it is recommended to do this every day by reshuffling the deck.

Three Card Spread

The next one is the three card spread. After shuffling the deck, you take out three cards one by one and put them in front of you. In a basic reading, this would mean your Past, Present, and Future. The first card represents all the elements and influences your past has had on your present. The second card is about you in the present—your current situation and mood. The third card does not show you the future but guides you toward figuring out what you need to do to let go of negativity and embrace your life goals.

This spread can also be interpreted in the following manner:

Instead of the past, present, and future, the variables can be:

- Set One — Body, Mind, Soul
- Set Two — Subconscious, Conscious, Superconscious
- Set Three — Inner Being, Needs, Methods

The Celtic Cross Spread

This can be thought of as the most detailed and analytical spread in the tarot layouts. Because it is a bit complex in arrangement and interpretation, this spread may appear daunting to beginners. However, once you get used to this, you will love it!

After shuffling, place the first card on the table. This represents you or the situation at hand. The second card goes across the first one. This card shows whatever problem or obstacle you are facing. The third, fourth, fifth, and sixth cards are arranged around the first two, with three and five directly below and above, and four and six to the left and right, respectively.

Three represents the situation itself—its basis and how you came to be in it. Four represents the events and mental state of the past, which led to the present situation. Five is for the present. Six indicates what can happen in the near future.

The next four cards are placed in a vertical column, with the seventh card at the bottom and the tenth at the top. Seven represents what abilities, talents, and skills you possess to deal with your situation. Eight is for the people in your life and what effect they have on your decisions and feelings. Nine represents any fears or anxieties you have and also shows you your hopes and desires. Ten represents the overall outcome of your reading.

The Five Card Spread

Shuffle the deck and pick out five cards. There are many layouts for this kind of spread but learn how to interpret the card number first.

- Card one — your question
- Card two — what you already know about the question or situation
- Card three — tries to point you towards the direction of a solution
- Card four — contains advice or pointers for the question
- Card five — the outcome of the question asked

If you wish to ask something related to the past or something bothering you about someone, try this method of interpretation:

- Card one — about your past

- Card two – about the recent events in the past
- Card three – conveys the present state
- Card four – guides you to the future realm
- Card five – outcome or far future

Here are two popular five card spreads:

Layout One: Five Card Cross

Put three cards in the middle and put one card above and one below it. You may designate it as three, five, and four in the middle and one and two above and below. Or, you may have two, one, and three in the middle and four and five above and below.

Layout Two: Relationship Spread

Place your first, fourth, and second card in the middle row and place the fifth card above and the third card below the line.

- Card one – your perspective and feelings about the relationship
- Card two – your partner's perspective about the relationship
- Card three – why you two got together in the first place; the very foundation of you as a couple
- Card four – present state of your relationship
- Card five – variable outcomes for the relationship

The Seven Card Spread (Horseshoe Spread)

The cards are arranged in a horseshoe formation, beginning with card one in the lower left corner and ending with card seven in the lower right corner.

- Card one – the events and feelings of the past, which are now influencing the present

- Card two — the present and the events, activities, feelings, desires, etc., associated with the current issue or question at hand

- Card three — hidden influences or under the surface currents that impact you. These are the unseen yet strongly felt feelings

- Card four — the person who is asking the question. This card reveals your entire being, attitude, personality, quirks, positive aspects, negative aspects, etc.

- Card five — how others influence you. Do they have a positive or negative effect on you? Why do you react to their words and actions? And how is that impacting your present?

- Card six — the course of action the person should take. It offers some possibilities and routes that the person might consider taking to reach their goal.

- Card seven — the outcome of all that the previous cards suggested. It is the culmination of the question and the arrival at an answer.

The Astrological Spread

This is an interesting spread, combining the zodiac signs and the tarot. In this spread, each card represents a zodiac sign and has its own meaning tied in with the tarot. There is no need to ask a question with this spread because the cards represent particular qualities and aspects of your life.

- Card one — Self

- Card two (Aries) — your current state of mind and how much you value yourself

- Card three (Taurus) — your current financial condition

- Card four (Gemini) — communication and travel

- Card five (Cancer) — family, parents, care, concern

- Card six (Leo) — productivity, pleasure, fierceness, competition
- Card seven (Virgo) — your health, partnerships, relationships
- Card eight (Libra) — marriage, love, romance, money, inheritance
- Card nine (Scorpio) — death, mystery, magnetism, emotional depth, secrets, philosophy
- Card ten (Sagittarius) — an attitude of giving, education, dreams
- Card eleven (Capricorn) — community, career, ambition
- Card twelve (Aquarius) — friendship, relationships, strong affinity to the inner self
- Card thirteen (Pisces) — fears, rebellious nature

In some interpretations, the centermost card, thirteen, is seen as the culmination of all the other cards and their meanings.

The Seven Day Spread

This is quite simple to read; all you have to do is shuffle the deck and place eight cards upon a surface, beginning with one and ending with seven. The last card, eight, can either go up or down. This spread tells you what your coming week is going to be like.

This is read from left to right. Each card stands for one day of the week. There is no intrinsic meaning attached to each position. Whatever cards you draw, they will be set according to this layout and read. One represents the current day; two represents the next day; three represents the day after; and so on.

The Six Month Spread

In this spread, four cards are used for insight into the next six months of your life.

The first card you choose is your Immediate Environment card. This card also signifies isolation, worries, insecurity, loss, and sadness. It symbolizes the loss of the skill to live life to the fullest and how you're struggling to make others understand you.

The second card is Exterior Influences. This section of the spread indicates communication, celebrations, success, happiness, reunion, affairs, gatherings, or any other influence you might have on your present.

The third card is of Past Circumstances. This represents illusions, imagination, dreams, choices, an inability to choose properly, selfishness on the person's part, or any other past circumstances that have prevented a present fruitful life.

The fourth card is Future Motivation. It reveals aspects that make you reach your goal. Your personality traits, prejudices, positive points, issues, attitude, and mental state—you get to know all of that in this section.

The Twelve Month Spread

This is another basic yet interesting spread. Shuffle the deck and select twelve cards from it. Place them in a circular position on the cloth or surface and try to remember what card you have placed in each position. Begin with card one and go clockwise.

- Card one (The Self) — you: your projection, perception, appearance, etc.
- Card two (Money) — your material wealth, finances, windfall, skills, worth, and potential

• Card three (Mental activities) — your intellect, grasping power, work, education, and career

• Card four (Emotions and feelings) — your emotional wellbeing, security, comfort level, new activities, home, and relationships

• Card five (Creativity) — your artistic ability, affairs of the heart, your relaxation activities, etc.

• Card six (Daily routine) — what you do in a day, your routine activities, job, recreation, colleagues, friends, and family

• Card seven (Work) — business matters, work, career, partners, work ethic, and business practices

• Card eight (Possessions) — your money, jewelry, inheritance, wills, bonds, shares, and any other precious commodity

• Card nine (Education) — studies, higher studies, stipends, internship, travel, and long-distance travel

• Card ten (Reputation) — your reputation in public, how people perceive you, your contributions toward other lesser fortunate people, and people in your family

• Card eleven (Goals) — your dreams, goals, wishes, and vision for the future

• Card twelve (Spirituality) — your innate psychic ability, dreams, escape mechanism, and spiritual growth

Conclusion

Congratulations on reaching the end of this book. Hopefully, you had a good time studying the various facets and aspects of divination.

A word to the wise, divination is still a budding field. While prevalent all over and practiced since ancient times, you still need to study and understand the divination methods completely and be open to learning at all times. Your intuition is all you need to guide you toward the right path. Do not lose sight of it, and do not ignore your gut feeling about anyone or anything. Ultimately, it is your thoughts, feelings, and intuition that will keep you on the right path—no book or person can do that for you. You need to ask questions, interpret the answers after looking at all aspects, and then decide on a course of action for yourself. Sure, there may be books and people to help you out but remember you are your own true friend.

All the methods given in the book are fun to try out and experiment with but do not get carried away by the answers you get. Take them at face value and try to keep improving yourself. It is not always necessary to absolutely believe the outcome predicted by the cards or runes or any other method. They are just guiding tools; they will certainly not predict the future with certainty. You can make your future better by making the present count. That is the lesson you must take away from this book. Please do not fall prey to unscrupulous people out there who will scam you and rob you of your peace of mind.

Trust yourself and live life to the fullest! The universe will definitely help you on your journey if your intentions are good.

Here's another book by Mari Silva that you might like

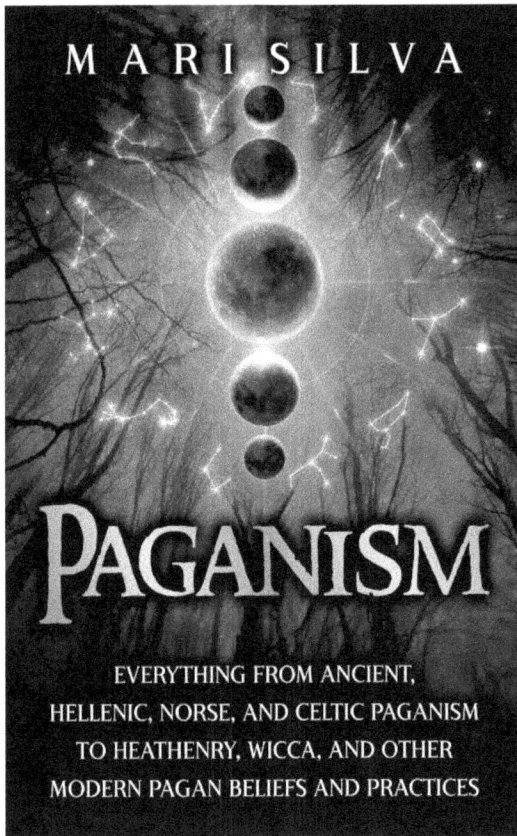

MARI SILVA

PAGANISM

EVERYTHING FROM ANCIENT,
HELLENIC, NORSE, AND CELTIC PAGANISM
TO HEATHENRY, WICCA, AND OTHER
MODERN PAGAN BELIEFS AND PRACTICES

Your Free Gift (only available for a limited time)

Thanks for getting this book! If you want to learn more about various spirituality topics, then join Mari Silva's community and get a free guided meditation MP3 for awakening your third eye. This guided meditation mp3 is designed to open and strengthen ones third eye so you can experience a higher state of consciousness. Simply visit the link below the image to get started.

https://spiritualityspot.com/meditation

Bibliography

Arnold, Kim. "10 Fascinating Facts about Tarot: Ten Tantalising Tidbits of Tarot Trivia!"

Hay House, Inc. November 30, 2018.

https://www.healyourlife.com/10-fascinating-facts-about-tarot

Cafe Astrology.com "The Elements in Astrology."

https://cafeastrology.com/natal/elements-astrology.html

Café Astrology. "What is Astrology?"
https://cafeastrology.com/whatisastrology.html

The Cut. "A Beginner's Guide to Tarot Cards." April 27, 2020.

https://www.thecut.com/article/tarot-cards.html

The Cut. "What Is Your Life-Path Number?" May 14, 2020.

https://www.thecut.com/article/life-path-number.html

Decoz, Hans. "Numerology's Master Numbers 11 – 22 – 33."
Hans Decoz and World Numerology LLC.
https://www.worldnumerology.com/numerology-master-numbers.htm

Divination Foundation. "A Short History of Divination." May 16, 2007.

https://divination.com/a-short-history-of-divination/

Garis, Mary Grace. "How to Read a Natal Chart—Planets, Symbols, and All." Well+Good

 LLC. March 31, 2020.

https://www.wellandgood.com/how-to-read-natal-chart/

Gilbert, Robert Andrew. "Divination: religion." Encyclopedia Britannica. February 16, 2001. https://www.britannica.com/topic/divination

Hurst, Katherine. "Numerology: What is Numerology? And How Does it Work?" The Law

Of Attraction by Greater Minds. December 18, 2017.

https://www.thelawofattraction.com/what-is-numerology/

Israelsen, James. "55 Celestial Facts about the Zodiac | Fact Retriever LLC. September 11,

2020. https://www.factretriever.com/zodiac-facts

Kahn, Nina. "Your Guide To The Planets In Astrology & How They Affect You." Bustle.

July 24, 2020.

https://www.bustle.com/life/how-each-planets-astrology-directly-affects-every-zodiac-sign-13098560

Mastering the Zodiac. "How to Read a Birth Chart.. in Minutes!" February 19, 2016.

https://masteringthezodiac.com/how-to-read-a-birth-chart/

Linder, Jean. "Tarot Spreads You Need Right Now." Kelleemaize.

https://www.kelleemaize.com/post/tarot-spreads-you-need-right-now

Lovejoy, Bess. "10 Historical Divination Methods for Predicting the Future." Mental Floss. June 12, 2019 https://www.mentalfloss.com/article/585258/historical-divination-methods-predict-future

Newcombe, Rachel. "Rune Guide - An Introduction to using the Runes." Holistic Shop.

https://www.holisticshop.co.uk/articles/guide-runes

Psychic Library, LLC. "Astrological Tarot Spread."

https://psychiclibrary.com/astrological-tarot-spread/

The Rune Site. "Casting layouts and spreads." http://www.therunesite.com/casting-layouts-and-spreads/

Sons of Vikings. "Viking Runes Guide | Runic Alphabet Meanings | Norse / Nordic

Letters." February 28, 2017.

https://sonsofvikings.com/blogs/history/viking-runes-guide-runic-alphabet-meanings-nordic-celtic-letters

Tarot.com Staff. "The Major Arcana Tarot Card Meanings." Tarot.com. March 3, 2021.

https://www.tarot.com/tarot/cards/major-arcana

Tarot.com Staff. "The Minor Arcana: Meanings Behind the Number Cards." February 3,

2021. https://www.tarot.com/tarot/meaning-of-numbers-in-minor-arcana

Time Nomads. "Elder Futhark Runes Cheat Sheet." January 11, 2020. https://www.timenomads.com/elder-futhark-alphabet-cheat-sheet/

Tracey, Ashley. "What Does Your Sun, Moon, and Rising Sign Really Mean?" Mindbody,

Inc. April 15, 201

https://explore.mindbodyonline.com/blog/wellness/what-does-your-sun-moon-and-rising-sign-really-mean

Wigington, Patti. "What Is Rune Casting? Origins and Techniques." Learn Religions.

January 31, 2020.

 https://www.learnreligions.com/rune-casting-4783609

Wille. "11 Popular Tarot Spreads for Beginners and Advanced readers." A LITTLE

SPARK OF JOY. December 23, 2020.

https://www.alittlesparkofjoy.com/easy-tarot-spreads/

yourchineseastrology.com. "Chinese Palmistry."

https://www.yourchineseastrology.com/palmistry/

www.ingramcontent.com/pod-product-compliance
Lightning Source LLC
Chambersburg PA
CBHW071859090426
42811CB00004B/667